CONSPIRACY THEORY CULTURE

CONSPIRACY THEORY CULTURE

The Interviews: Volume 5

ALAN R. WARREN
DR. JOSEPH USCINSKI

Copyright

Conspiracy Theory Culture: The Interviews
Written by Alan R. Warren
Published by House of Mystery

Copyright @ 2021 by Alan R. Warren

Cover design, formatting, layout, and editing by Evening Sky Publishing Services

Published in United States of America
ISBN (Paperback): 978-1-989980-28-6
ISBN (eBook): 978-1-989980-27-9

CONTENTS

Foreword

BY DR. JOSEPH USCINSKI

As of late, there has been much written about conspiracy theories: who believes them, why, and to what effect. Most certainly, the Trump presidency and the COVID-19 pandemic have brought the dangers of conspiracy theories front and center. Beliefs inform actions, and when people believe conspiracy theories, they may act on them with deadly results.

During the pandemic, conspiracy theories surrounding COVID-19 led some people to forgo best practices, like hand washing, mask-wearing, and social distancing. Other people, fearing we were being attacked by a bioweapon, hoarded vital goods creating product shortages. In either case, beliefs led to actions, and the actions were detrimental.

Following the election of Joe Biden to the presidency, many people clung to the belief that Donald Trump had indeed won a second term but was being cheated by a corrupt voting system. Some of the people who believed this stormed the Capitol Building on January 6th, 2021, precipitating five needless deaths. Just the online chatter in the wake of the "Capitol Riot" was enough to get Congress to suspend its business on March 4th in fear of further conspiracy theory-induced violence. Indeed, like other ideas, when taken too far, conspiracy theories can be dangerous.

With that said, and when not acted upon or used to form a worldview, conspiracy theories can be harmless fun. They can be a form of storytelling. There is something uniquely intriguing about a good conspiracy theory. They tell tales of heroes, villains, and alternative realities. Conspiracy theories represent secret knowledge: true or not, you are not supposed to know this theory; you are not supposed to think in this way; you are not supposed to question. There is something very fun about having supposed insider knowledge; to know something special. Because of their entertainment value, you can find conspiracy theories everywhere. They populate our television programming, the movies, and are all over the internet. But there is something very unique when conspiracy theories traverse the radio waves – it's like combining chocolate and peanut butter. Conspiracy theories, of course, make for great movies and TV series, but over the radio waves – alone with just a voice from afar – conspiracy theories are at their best.

At no point in my life have I ever believed that the earth was flat. But some people do think this, and they will go to great lengths to prove it to others. The fascinating part of the contemporary Flat Earth group is their ability to gather "evidence" for their claims and weave that evidence into grand theories. For Flat-Earthers, everyone but them is in on the hoax: geographers, governments, airline pilots, astronauts, mapmakers, and the globe industry. Everyone is covering up the earth's true shape for some reason. Maybe it's to hide biblical truth, or maybe it's to trick humanity into misunderstanding the true nature of our universe. These are certainly fascinating ideas, and hearing about them over the radio waves only makes the ideas more intriguing, despite their implausibility. As some people say, Flat Earth theories are famous all over the globe.

The same goes for many other conspiracy theories that Al has entertained on *House of Mystery* over the years. Implausibility doesn't make conspiracy theories less entertaining. What if the moon landing was faked? Who would have been involved, how could they have pulled it off, and why? How could it have been kept secret for so long? While I do not subscribe to moon landing conspiracy theories (only 6% of Americans do), they are, for me, some of the most entertaining. What if famed movie direction Stanley Kubrick was involved, as some argue? What if the lunar landing was faked as part of a Cold War ploy to trick the Soviets? What if the earth is encapsulated by a celestial lid? I am not convinced of any of these ideas, but hearing the arguments of the believers tells much about human psychology.

Like the moon landing, historical events make great fodder for conspiracy theories, but the moon landing is not the only event attracting alternative accounts. The idea that Hitler escaped the bunker at the end of World War II is as fascinating as the idea of a faked moon landing or flat earth. What if the infamous leader of the Third Reich escaped? How could we know if that was true? Some argue that Hitler escaped to Argentina, where he lived out his days. Others argue that he amassed a new military force on Antarctica, awaiting the right time to make his return. Similarly, what if President Franklin Roosevelt had allowed the Pearl Harbor attacks to happen? This argument has been floating around since the attack and has been endorsed by numerous high-profile leaders and activists. Of course, it has never been substantially shown to be true. And, still to this day, there are many questioning Princess Diana's death, who was tragically killed in a car crash more than twenty years ago. Some blame Queen Elizabeth; others blame amorphous shadowy interests. The truth may be more mundane than the theories, but the theories are entertaining, nonetheless. When the imagination is allowed to wander, the possibilities are indeed endless.

I have had the pleasure to work on *House of Mystery* with Al Warren for the last few years. I first started out doing a ten-minute weekly countdown of the top internet conspiracy theories each week. For about a year, I would list off the trending conspiracy theories; I was always shocked by the diversity of the ideas that got traction. For nearly a month, there seemed to be a scare about a fictional planet (Nibiru) that was headed along a collision course for earth. Luckily for all of us, either Nibiru didn't exist, or it missed us, sparing our lives. I am going to go with the former over the latter.

I was eventually "promoted" to doing hour-long shows interviewing authors of new and interesting books. The guests that Al booked always fascinated me – they ranged from scientists and doctors to film producers and paranormal investigators. One week we would interview guests who argued that Jesus never existed, and then the next week, we would welcome a guest who claimed to have found Jesus's tomb. Though sometimes productive and sometimes not, the conversations were always interesting. Al is great at picking interesting people who like to talk and have a story to tell. In this collection, Al has assembled some of his greatest interviews discussing conspiracy theories.

I'm a pollster and spend most of my days analyzing people's responses to questions about conspiracy theories. In short, I work mostly with data and don't spend that much time talking through all of the various conspiracy theories with the people who develop them, improve upon them, and believe them. But, my work with Al on the *House of Mystery* has allowed me to do just that. I got to see how people's minds worked, how they responded to questions, and how they dealt with pushback. Sometimes guests are open to being questioned; other times, they are less amenable to stern questioning.

House of Mystery is, therefore, very much an exploration not just into ideas but into the people who promote and cling to those ideas. I am sure you will find this collection of some of the best interviews from the *House of Mystery* as fascinating as I have.

Introduction

The *House of Mystery Radio Show* has been on the air for ten years now, broadcasting in over a dozen cities in the United States, including KKNW 1150 A.M. Seattle/Tacoma, KCAA 106.5 F.M. Los Angeles/102.3 F.M. Riverside/1050 A.M. Palm Springs. I started the show to find out as much information on the world's mysteries in areas of Crime, Science, Religion, history, paranormal, and more. Like most people, I have heard stories, rumors, and read books or watched documentaries on television, but would seldom hear one direct answer to a question.

Throughout my time recording interviews, I sought out people who had themselves researched a subject enough to have written a book or created a documentary, or even people involved in the event or topic that would have first-hand knowledge.

In most cases, the strange thing was that there was a popular or mainstream idea about what happened, one reported at the time of the event, but then there was an alternative idea. Most writers who had books or shows that did well quite often disagreed with the current theory and would accuse the media of faking the story and hiding the truth from everyone.

An example would be "Who shot JFK?" There has been a well-known theory reported by different government agencies and news media that most people in America have come to accept as the truth. But since the original Warren Report on JFK's assassination, there have been hundreds of theories promoted by many authors and lots of research completed.

In this series, we review the most accepted explanation on the topic. Then, we follow up with each of the alternative theories presented during our interviews with the person or people reporting them. There will be no committed answer at the end of the book. Our goal is to provide a concise review of the extraordinary things we learned during the show's interviews.

Each book in this series lays out the topic's details and then follows up with what we've learned from each guest. This book, like the others in the House of Mystery Radio Show Interviews Series, does not attempt to solve the case but only review it. It is an excellent reference for researchers and a good overview for people who don't know the topic well. Similar to the other volumes in this series, only the highlights of each interview will be included.

All of these interviews, and more, are available to listen to on my website: *www.alanrwarren.com/hom-podcast-episodes*

So, the world is flat? I thought I had heard it all! The first thought that I had was this is silly, and I'm not going to waste any time on it. Being on the radio, I have to select the best possible show. One that is interesting and avoids as much crap as possible. Not only for the listeners but also for the network and stations that play our show. But conspiracies have always held my interest, and I'm not exactly sure why.

Like most people, while living my life, I have heard lots of them. Probably the oldest and most popular are the JFK assassination theories. These I find the most interesting because it's about an event that we all know *happened for sure*, and even *what happened*. But what we don't know, or at least we don't want to believe, is that Lee Harvey Oswald did it, and he did it alone. There is definite room for doubt. The *House of Mystery Radio Show* has had lots of episodes covering the many theories about that event and others like it.

This particular book isn't going to look at those types of conspiracy theories. Those are far too large in scope and deserve their own book, which I have previously released. (See "Also in The House of Mystery Interview Series" Section of this book) Volume 5 of the *House of Mystery Interviews Series* will focus on theories that go against the scientific facts that we have learned over many generations of the human race. They go against some of the most basic of psychics that we all live by and never give them a second thought.

I am going to stay away from anything considered paranormal as they are also huge projects in scope, and each area, such as U.F.O's or Ghosts, needs to have its own book with several interviews to give you as much information as possible from as many angles as possible.

As with the others in this series, this book will cover the most popular conspiracies – the ones that have gained lots of ground in the media and on the internet. Some of them have celebrity followers as well. During the interviews, I show the guests the most respect and really try to find out their reasoning for believing what they do and also how they developed their beliefs.

The Earth Is Flat

The Conspiracy Theory

First up is the Flat Earth Theory. This has really gained attention in the last ten years and is one of those theories that even has celebrities speaking out about it. Shaquille O'Neal claimed the Earth was flat on his podcast called *The Big Podcast with Shaq* claiming that when he drove from Florida to California, the world seemed flat to him. Obviously, even if you have a lot of money, it doesn't mean that you're smart.

In February of 2017, NBA player Kyle Irving made a comment about there being no evidence of the world being round with two other NBA players on a podcast. Rapper B.o.B. composed a song, "Flatline," in which he claims the Earth is flat. Later in 2016, he accepted a membership in the Flat Earth Society. On Twitter, he later posted a picture with cities in the background that was about 16 miles apart and captioned it with "Where's the curve?" These were only a few of the celebrities making waves talking about the Flat Earth Conspiracy Theory.

The Flat Earth Society has over 213,000 people now following it on Facebook and 93,000 on Twitter.

In 1956, Samuel Shenton created the International Flat Earth Research Society as a successor to the Universal Zetetic Society from his home in Dover, England. Shenton died in 1971. Charles K. Johnson inherited part of Shenton's library from Shenton's wife and established and became president of the International Flat Earth Research Society of America and Covenant People's Church in California. Over the next three decades, under his leadership, the Flat Earth Society grew to a reported 3,500 members. Flat Earth Society recruited members by speaking against the US government and all its agencies, particularly NASA. Much of the society's literature in its early days focused on interpreting the Bible to mean that the Earth is flat, although they did try to offer scientific explanations and evidence.

In a 1984 flyer, Charles K. Johnson wrote:

"Historical accounts and spoken history tell us the Land part may have been square, all in one mass at one time, then as now, the Magnetic North being the Center. Vast cataclysmic events and shaking no doubt broke the land apart, divided the land to be our present continents or islands as they exist today. One thing we know for sure about this world...the known inhabited world is Flat, Level, a Plain World."

The Flat Earth Society's most recent planet model is that humanity lives on a disc, with the North Pole at its center and a 150-foot-high wall of ice, Antarctica, at the outer edge. The resulting map resembles the symbol of the United Nations, which Johnson used as evidence for his position.

In this model, the Sun and Moon are each 32 miles in diameter.

Modern "Flat-Earthers" generally embrace some form of conspiracy theory out of the necessity of explaining why major institutions such as governments, media outlets, schools, scientists, and airlines all assert that the world is a sphere. Instead of the internet and social media making it harder to promote such theories simply because of the available information online, it instead makes it easier to spread disinformation and attract others to erroneous ideas.

Not long before the writing of this book, on Saturday, February 22, 2020, 64-year-old "Mad"

Mike Hughes was killed when he crash-landed his steam-powered rocket shortly after take-off near Barstow in the desert in San Bernardino County, California. Hughes was a member of the Flat Earth community, and in numerous interviews, he had stated that the goal of his rocket launches was to prove that the planet was not spherical. A former stuntman, Hughes had done two rocket launches prior to his death, one in 2014 and one in 2018, from which he emerged without major incident.[1]

Interview with Mark Sargent

By 2018, the documentary *Behind the Curve* was released, which followed Mark Sargent, a prominent member of the Flat Earth Society, in his attempt to prove his theory. So, what better person to go to ask for an interview on how he knew the world was flat than Mark Sargent.

Q. Let's start out with what you think the Earth is. I mean as in shape, size, and any other details that you can explain to the listeners, so we can understand it.

A. Yes, a lot of people are going to be listening and going, "What in the world is he talking about?" We are talking about literally a Flat Earth / enclosed world / enclosed system. There are various references I'll throw out there. If you don't know *The Truman Show* with Jim Carey from 1998, or *Dark City*, or *Under the Dome*, the currently running television series that Steven Spielberg is producing and Stephen King wrote. If you don't know any of those references, then what you're looking at is something really like out of the Old Testament, Genesis 1-6, the firmament.

Then God said, *"Let there be a firmament in the midst of the waters, and let it divide the waters from the waters." Thus, God made the firmament and divided the waters which were under the firmament from the waters which were above the firmament; and it was so. And God called the firmament Heaven. So, the evening and the morning were the second day."*

This is a flat world that isn't a sphere. It's actually an enclosed system. So, if you take a globe and put your hand on the North Pole, and you flatten it like a dinner plate, it becomes circular, and then you cover it with some sort of dom'ish structure, and that's really it.

The North Pole is at the center of this dinner plate, and the continents are spread out organically out towards the edges. The only thing that really makes it different from a globe in terms of what you're looking at, other than it's not spherical, is that Antarctica isn't a continent. Because that's the first question, "Wouldn't the water fall off the edges?" It's like, no, because Antarctica goes all the way around. It isn't a continent like Australia, with 13 million square miles of ice. It is an Antarctic coastline that spreads around. Think of it as a rim on a dinner plate all the way around. That part we at least know is true. At least as far as the Antarctic coastline, I mean. It slopes up 200 feet high. It's made of ice, and then, once you get over the top of that thing, it slopes up to almost two miles high and even higher in some places.

If you still haven't figured out the visual, I know you're listening to the radio. If you still haven't figured out the visual of it, look at the U.N. flag. The design was created in 1946. That's pretty much what we look at. The U.N. flag is identical, give or take, the scale is probably going to be off because we just don't know the exact scale, but the continent layout is pretty much what the Flat Earth map uses, and the United States Geological survey.

Q. So, how thick do you suggest the Earth is?

A. That's a great question. I'm so glad that you asked that. I'll come back with another question, "How thick do you think the Earth is?" Because mainstream science says, it's 4,000 miles down to the center of the Earth. I go, that's fantastic, so you've drilled that far? Do you have cameras down there? No. Well, okay, 1,000 miles then?

No. 100 miles? Ten? The deepest hole ever drilled by any corporation, non-military at least, publicly in the world is eight miles.

The Soviets tried for years, and they got down to about eight miles – that's 12 kilometers. They stayed there. They could not get past eight miles for whatever reason. Yet, mainstream science will come back and tell you, and we've all seen those cross-sections of the globe where it goes from red to orange to yellow to that milky white center. Where did you come up with that map? It's because mainstream science won't put a question mark in the middle of that globe map.

The short answer is we don't know how thick it is. We don't know how thick we are on it, you know, where we are now. If I had to take a guess, I'd say it was way less than the Earth's thickness, you know, 4,000 miles to the center, 8,000 miles all the way across. Because we can't go down any further than that, which is very suspicious to me.

Q. What do you think is on the other side?

A. Wow, that's wide open. It could be anything, to be honest, if you're talking about efficiency because this really leads into some bigger questions, which is okay. If this place was created and it's flat, then the whole question of intelligent design comes straight into the forefront.

Okay, if it was flat, which means that it was built, and it was created. Therefore, there's your creator. If a creator, a divine power, or an advanced civilization, I'm kind of blurring the lines there on the same thing, created this place, there could be another one on the flip side of it.

It could be a double-sided coin, where you have an enclosed system on one side and an enclosed system on the other.

Q. What's your estimate on how high the dome is above us?

A. That's a tough one because we, the tests that were done from late 1958 until 1962 between the Soviet Union and the United

States, when they were putting atomic weapons on the tops of rockets, and they were firing basic straight up for four years. We know it's at least 400 kilometers high. At least publicly, that's the tests that they have shown. So, if you want perspective on this, take a half-dollar and put it on the table and then take a salad bowl maybe, eight inches across the glass, put it over the top of it, that's what we're kind of looking at. I don't think it's like a snow globe arc, but it's more like a shallow sports stadium. Art imitates life in this case. The top of the dome could be several thousand miles high. It's really a giant planetarium.

Q. The dome itself, is it transparent? There is the Sun, the Moon, and on a clear night, there appear to be stars. So, is that real, or is it painted on the dome?

A. The latter. I think it's painted in. But I've got to address several things here. People are going to ask, "Are the stars real?" Yes, the stars are real. Am I killing astrology? No, I am not. The stars still move across the sky. We can all see that.

However, in this sort of system, the stars, again like a planetarium, the stars, the Moon, and the Sun, are just really very well rendered images. People are going to say that the planets are round, so doesn't that make us round? Yes, well, they look round, but you got to remember that the whole point of this illusion is to make us seem like we're in a round or spherical thing.

The only people that show us really good pictures of all the planets are NASA, and we'll get into that later. What makes this different than a normal planetarium, though, a normal planetarium you can show moonlight, sunlight, and stars all in one system. You can project the whole thing on the ceiling. But with this, it appears that the Sun and the Moon are three-dimensional objects. Inside this, you know, like hanging and spinning around no different than a mobile above a child's crib. Where the Moon and the Sun appear to be the same size, especially when the Moon goes in front of the Sun, but they're inside here with us. They may be less than 50 miles across and maybe a few thousand miles high. The Sun is just one big incandescent lightbulb, and the Moon is a giant nightlight. Ask me about that later because the Moon's light properties, we found out in the last few months, are very different than what we've been told.

Q. So, we are not a sphere, and we are not doing as we are told, so what are we physically doing? Are we spinning? Are we rotating? Are we traveling?

A. This answer is going to kill some listeners. We are not doing anything.

All the motion, because you have to remember mainstream science will tell you that the Earth is spinning at 1,100 miles an hour, and that it's traveling around the Sun at 60,000 miles an hour, and that our Solar System is moving through the Galaxy at like a half-a-million miles an hour when you look it up those numbers vary. But that's a lot of motion happening in a lot of different places. Plus, you've got the Moon spinning around us, apparently. All these things should be happening.

Yet, in the flat model, nothing is happening. Literally, we could be on someone's desk or on a much bigger surface. Again, no different than a planetarium. When you go in there, you're not moving. The premise of what I put forward starting in February of 2015, was "What if you could build a planetarium?" I know it's going to sound like something out of the Twilight Zone or very science fiction. The truth is often stranger than fiction. But what if you could build a planetarium? What if you had the technology to build one thousands-of-miles wide and at least hundreds of miles high? How many people could you fool in that system? Let's say that they were born into it. Let's face it if the planetarium were big enough, and you were born into it, you would believe basically anything anybody told you. Because how could you test it? How would you know?

How long could you keep civilization in the dark, so to speak, from finding out where they really were? It appears that in our case, we're pushing about 5,000 years, give or take. This is also what every tribe, every culture, every religion believed in for thousands of years. It was only 500 years ago that the whole Copernicus Heliocentric model was produced.

Copernican heliocentrism is the name given to the astronomical model developed by Nicolaus Copernicus and published in 1543. This model positioned the Sun at the center of the Universe, motionless, with Earth and the other planets orbiting around it in circular paths, modified by epicycles, and at uniform speeds.[2]

So, we've been riding that for the last 500 years, and now our technology has reached a point where detection, high-speed internet, and HD, basically camera technology, high-speed internet, and social media, ruined the whole thing because now we're comparing notes. And as of 2015, this whole thing is starting to break down.

I'll give you an example. When you type into Google the term "Flat Earth" last year, you may have gotten maybe 50,000 relevant hits. You type that same thing in today, as of this morning, and it's 4.7 million hits.

Q. So, I'm sure the listeners would next like to know who is doing this? Who would be hiding this?

A. From the authority standpoint, and when I say authority, I mean the "powers that be" – the super-rich, the royals, and the governments. Imagine if this world was eventually supposed to find out eventually. We were supposed to figure out where the edge was and where the ceiling was. It was supposed to be a natural process. The governments of the Soviet Union and the United States seem to have figured it out back in 1956. More specifically, during "Operation Deep Freeze" between 1955 and 1956. They were the ones that decided it would be too disruptive to civilization. And I won't go into the religion. But religion would play an angle here because you are talking about intelligent design. They decided, let's just spend the money and seal off the upper edge and the outer edge, and let's see how long we can hide this thing.

So, yes, the Soviet Union and the United States are responsible for hiding it.

Q. How does that work as we get new people in the government? You know, from Kennedy to Obama? When they're running for government, they don't really know?

A. Most people don't. But with some secrets, and I'm not going to go into too many other conspiracies during the show, but everyone knows what they are. With most conspiracies, you might inform people. Even Eisenhower didn't know, for example, that Area 51 was built. He had to actually force his way in to see the place.

Presidents, you don't have to tell them if you don't want to. Putin might be a different character. But in this case, because it's such a big secret, it's really less is more: the less people that know, the better. So, compartmentalize everything. So, any wrench-turners at NASA, or anyone who's building things for satellites, they don't need to know. Airline pilots, they don't know. Nobody knows. Because it's too big, it's so big, and it's right in front of your face. I mean, heck, it was right in front of my face 15 years ago, literally staring me in the face, and I couldn't see the forest through the trees. Almost nobody knows. Your secret societies, take your pick on who you want to name on those, maybe even those know but only at the highest levels. But you've got to be way up on the food chain to know this thing.

Q. What is the point of hiding it?

A. What I have learned more than anything about the rules of power and authority is that if there's a chance civilization may grab the torches and the pitchforks and run through the streets, burning things and killing each other, you're not going to roll those dice.

Let's say all of a sudden they said, "By the way, you are in an enclosed world. Here's the edge, pretty much the handprint of God." Let's say the U.N. announces that tomorrow. The wave of what would happen, and it wouldn't happen overnight, but the wave of things that would happen, would be as follows:

The education systems would be turned upside down, especially the physical sciences – everything from high school through to the Ph.D. process. You'd have to rewrite so many things; astrophysics and astronomy don't even exist anymore. Geology, hydrology, archeology, biology have to be rewritten from the ground up with a new model.

The big five religions: Christianity, Islam, Hinduism, Buddhism, and Judaism, all get their holy grail, so to speak, instantly overnight. There's going to be a backlash against science, which would be extremely upsetting.

The big thing for the individual person, a lot of people say, "Who cares if it's round or flat, I still got to go to my job in the morning, and it sucks." But now you're going to be driving to your job, and you're going to have this strange feeling that someone's been looking over your shoulder your entire life. If you want to call it God, or you want to call it the big eye in the sky, or an advanced civilization, whatever, you're going to act differently. You combine all of these things, the powers that be, they're not going to make that call. They'd think about it for about ten seconds. Until they started looking at the stuff, I was mentioning, and then they are going to say we're not going to do this now. Not even in the 50s, it would have been tough to do.

Q. Are all of the other countries involved in the secret as well?

A. Most countries don't even know. Not even at the highest level, I think, because why would they? It's not even the countries that matter. It would be things like the oil companies. You look at the Antarctica Treaty, which was put in place in 1959. That sealed off all countries from doing any corporate work down there for all time. It's the longest-running treaty in all of history, and nobody knows about it. You can look it up. It's on Wiki. Not only are they not allowed to go down there, but they're also not allowed to talk about it. Even though Admiral Bird went on television in 1954 and said, "Oh yeah, the place is made out of money. It's got oil. It's got coal, uranium, and minerals." All the countries that are rebuilding from World War II would want to get in there, and they just sealed it off.

Antarctic Treaty (Dec. 1, 1959), the agreement signed by 12 nations. The primary purpose of the Antarctic Treaty is to ensure "in the interests of all mankind that Antarctica shall continue forever to be used exclusively for peaceful purposes and shall not become the scene or object of international discord." To this end, it prohibits military activity, except in support of science. Antarctica is Earth's only continent without a native human population.[3]

So, if you're the head of Exxon and you want to go down there, you're not allowed to go down there to do any oil work. You're not even allowed to lobby for it. That was the big turning point for me as to how that is even possible. Money is the backstage pass for everything. You're not even allowed to run an ad in the *New York Times* saying how great it is for Exxon to go down to Antarctica.

You can't tell me the U.N. has that much power. They don't. If they want to start fracking in your backyard in your neighborhood, they can do that. They can get in the national parks.

Q. You mentioned pilots earlier. If I take a plane to Hawaii, then to Rio, how does it work that the pilots do not realize that they are flying over a flat rather than spherical planet?

A. There are several reasons. I have talked to quite a few, including a flight instructor and a United States Airforce Officer. The pilots wouldn't know because when they fly, they're busy. Between the time they take off, and the time they land, they are checking a lot of things. When they're not checking a lot of things, most of the time, they are relying on autopilot, and autopilot relies on the GPS. The GPS was designed by the United States Department of Defense.

Don't think for a second that the GPS isn't in on this. Part of the GPS's job is to keep people from going in certain directions where they're not supposed to be going. So, no, they don't notice when things get really weird in the southern hemisphere. And by that, I mean, flight routes.

Flight routes in the southern hemisphere make very little sense, especially if you're flying south to south. So, if you're like going from Rio to Sydney, you try to look for non-stops. There'll be 50 connecting flights, and there'll be maybe one non-stop, maybe. There are like five non-stops in the entire southern hemisphere from anywhere to anywhere.

But the routes are all over the place. Somebody said the routes are wrong. The routes only make sense if the Earth was flat. Try to book a flight from anywhere in

South America to anywhere in Australia and see where the planes go. Look where those connections go. They go way up north. Why is a flight from Rio to Sydney going through Los Angeles? Or Dallas? Or San Francisco? The cost of fuel, the price of fuel per pound is what the airlines base their profit margins on. Yes, you're picking up people, but not for those types of routes.

Q. Wouldn't the pilots and airlines question that themselves?

A. Good point. If you're a pilot, and it takes a lot of time to be a pilot, especially in the commercial airline world, you've got to stay squeaky clean, especially on what you say and do.

But more than that, this is such a huge leap of faith. This whole concept is so far down in the checklist. Let's say you're a pilot, and you're curious and bored, and then you're looking through the maps and charts, and you start thinking that the fuel consumption is wrong, the distances seem wrong, and the route seems wrong. Why does the GPS drop off in those three oceans entirely when you get over water?

If you go down your list of things that you are curious about, are you really going to get to the point where you say the map is wrong? The only way the map can be right is if the Earth is flat. Even if you came to that conclusion if you're a pilot, who are you going to tell? Are you going to go to the airline? Are you going to go to your supervisor? If you go and do that, then you're not a pilot anymore. You might as well tell them that you were chased by a UFO. If you're a pilot, and you tell them that you were chased by a UFO, then you're benched. You'll have an office job for the rest of your career if you even have a career.

Q. What about the satellites and GPS? Do they really exist?

A. I've got to come back with another question, and I don't mean to insult any of the listeners. Who told you that there were satellites, to begin with?

The same people who told you we went to the moon six times and never had any problems went through the Van Allen Radiation Belts. And nobody died of radiation poisoning? Nobody got radiation sickness. The capsules were never contaminated. And they don't tell you which shielding they used. There are only two types of shielding you can use for radiation shielding, and one of them is lead, which we all wear at the dentist's office. Or there's gold, but they don't talk about it. So, you've got to abandon everything, and that is why so many people get upset.

The Van Allen belts are not actually part of our atmosphere. They're well beyond it, extending hundreds of miles outwards into space. There are two, both donut-shaped rings surrounding our planet and are a consequence of our planet's magnetic field. The Space Shuttle typically orbited at the height of 190 miles to 330 miles above the surface, and the International Space Station orbits at the height of somewhere between 205 and 270 miles above the surface of the Earth.

The Van Allen belts are a kind of trap for charged particles like protons and electrons. They're held in place by the magnetic field of the Earth, and so they trace the shape of the magnetic field itself. The problem with the Van Allen belts lies not in them being impassable but in the charged particles they contain.

Charged particles are damaging to human bodies, but the amount of damage done can range from none to lethal, depending on the energy those particles deposit, the density of those particles, and the length of time you spend being exposed to them.

The density of the Van Allen belts is well known (from sending unscrewed probes through them), and there are hotspots you can definitely avoid. In particular, the innermost belt is a rather tightly defined region, and it was possible to stay out of it for the trip to the Moon. The second belt is much larger and harder to avoid, but there are still denser regions to avoid. For the Apollo trips, we wanted to send the astronauts through a sparse region of the belts and to try and get through them quickly. This was necessary in any case; the crafts had to make it to the Moon in a reasonable amount of time, and the shorter the trip, the less exposure to all sorts of radiation the astronauts would get.

In the end, it seemed that these tactics worked; the onboard dose counters for the Apollo missions registered average radiation doses to the skin of the astronauts of 0.38 rad. This is about the same radiation dose as getting two CT scans of your head, or half the dose of a single chest CT scan; not too bad, though not something you should do every week.[4]

I'm going as far as to say that the entire NASA from 1958 right up until today, the entire purpose was to hide the world that you live in. They've done an admirable job in some ways, but they're limited to the age of the special effects. If you have any doubt of that, look at the Apollo moon landing.

Q. So, you are saying all of NASA is involved? How can they get away with that?

A. This conspiracy is different from all the other conspiracies you've ever heard of. It's also the oldest one that everyone has heard of. But it's not like the "Manhattan Project" where we kept the atomic weapon program secret. That was thousands and thousands of people, and everyone knew it was going on, but they kept it a secret. Remember, there were only three television networks back then, so it's not like things could leak out that easily. You could control the media a lot more.

In this case, you don't need to tell the wrench-turners. One of my neighbors was Wayne Ottinger. He was like the garage mechanic for NASA. He knew all the astronauts from Gemini to Apollo on a first name basis. He knew nothing is what I'm getting at, and if you look at the time, why would you tell him anything? He was there to do a job, to build everything to do with rockets and get somebody to the Moon if you could do it.

Wayne Ottinger has more than fifty-five years of aerospace engineering and management experience, including positions with federal and state agencies, industry, consulting, and small business. His aerospace technology experience includes jet and rocket propulsion, flight-testing, engine control systems, ejection systems, energy conservation, and renewable energy sources. He was the Lunar Landing Training Vehicle Technical Director and Base Manager (Ellington Field LLTV Flight Test) for Bell Aerosystems Co. for the NASA Flight Research Center (now Armstrong Flight Research Center), he was Project Engineer (Flight Operations) for the Lunar Landing Research Vehicle and Propulsion Engineer for the X-15 Rocket Aircraft.[5]

Leave everybody out of the loop. I mean everyone in the control room and on the ground. The only people you really need in there are the telemetry guys. Those are the guys that have to create the data that's supposedly simulated and sent back to Earth from the program. If you want a record of that, just look at the movie

Capricorn One. It's about a guy that realized that the data didn't make sense, and they took care of that guy. He was killed.

Capricorn One – Three astronauts are about to launch into space on the first mission to Mars, but when a mechanical failure surfaces that would kill the three men, NASA removes them from the Capricorn One capsule. To prevent a public outcry, NASA launches the capsule unmanned and requires the astronauts to film fake mission footage in a studio. However, the plan is compromised when an ambitious journalist discovers the conspiracy.[6]

Anyone that was doing the telemetry would have to be in on it, the rest of NASA. I mean, 99.99 percent of them knew nothing, with the exception of one other group, which would have been the astronauts themselves. The one group of astronauts, nowadays, don't tell them. They know they're faking something, but they don't know why.

I think, with the Apollo crew, they told them why. "You're going to be faking some things, and it's a really important reason, and here's why." These guys were true-blue boy scout heroes. That's why they were so vetted.

Look at the International Space conference when they came back from Apollo 11. Those guys should have been pumped up with adrenalin for weeks. I mean, permanent smiles they should have had on their faces. They looked as if all their dogs had been shot. In fact, Neil (Armstrong) was cracking. He was even having a hard time getting his sentences out and ended up being a wreck. Most of these guys crawled into a bottle or hid from the public for years and years.

On July 20, 1969, Neil Armstrong and Apollo 11 Lunar Module pilot Buzz Aldrin became the first people to land on the Moon, and the next day they spent two and a half hours outside the Lunar Module Eagle spacecraft while Michael Collins remained in lunar orbit in the Apollo Command

Module Columbia. After he resigned from NASA in 1971, Armstrong taught in the Department of Aerospace Engineering at the University of Cincinnati until 1979. He served on the Apollo 13 accident investigation and on the Rogers Commission, which investigated the Space Shuttle Challenger disaster. He acted as a spokesman for several businesses and appeared in advertising for the automotive brand Chrysler starting in January 1979.[7]

Q. What about the pictures and films that we have from space?

A. That's an interesting one, and that was what got me going on this. From 1972 right up until June of 2015, there was only one picture of the Earth taken in full sunlight from space. You can look it up. This is not secret information. It was Apollo 17, taken in 1972, that we've all seen it in the textbooks. It shows the bottom part of Africa and all of Antarctica. There's no coincidence there. A lot of clouds with a big crescent shape on it, and that was the one they milked for 43 years. There should be ten thousand, or an unlimited amount of pictures, but there's only one.

As far as video of the Earth, there's zero. People will say they can see the ISS footage. I mean, the full Earth, rotating on its axis from space. The only one they made briefly claim to be the 1990 Galileo footage, which was dissected almost immediately, in fact, recently, by a Flat Earth guy. You watch the 24-hour spinning of it, and the weather doesn't change. The weather didn't morph or change in 24 hours. That's not even possible in 24 hours, and they even time-stamped it.

Anything you see now that came after 2014, I don't consider valid because it's all response to what we've been putting out there. We're the ones that said, "Where are the pictures of Earth from outer space?" Then, in June of 2015, they presented one. The White House tweeted it, then Neil DeGrasse Tyson retweeted it, and it's nothing but a whole bunch of clouds. It's even worse than the first one from 1972.

Q. Let's get into the Moon. What about the Earth having a shadow on the Moon, and there's a film of that? Eclipses?

A. Oh yeah, make no mistake about it, when I say you've got to throw out everything, I mean everything – not just the shadow, but the Blood Moon. The Blood Moon isn't possible. The shadow isn't possible on a Flat Earth because, technically, there is no Earth between the Sun and the Moon. The Sun and the Moon are right across from each other. Therefore, whatever images you see must be artificial. And if you think I'm kidding, look up two things on the internet when you get a chance.

The first thing is "Lunar Waves." You type that in anywhere, and you'll find a whole bunch of hits on that. Where there seems to be a resolution issue, a refresh rate issue, like a vertical hold issue on the Moon that we've only been able to detect on High-definition cameras recently.

The second one that you've got to look up is "moonlight is colder." I don't mean, and everyone that's listening will be thinking, of course, it's colder at night, but I don't mean that. The moonlight is generating some sort of refrigeration radiation. Everyone knows that when it's 100-degrees in the Sun, it's 90-degrees in the shade because the shade is blocking some of the Sun's radiation. But when you do the same thing in the moonlight, you can use a digital thermometer, you point it at something in the moonlight, and let's say it's 50 degrees, then you point it in the Moon shade, and it's 60 degrees.

But that's impossible. It can't be warmer in the shade because the Moon is reflecting some of the Sun's radiation. At least it should be a little bit warmer in the moonlight or even neutral. But we've seen stuff already on video that's up to 12 degrees colder. That's not possible unless the Moon is self-illuminated. Which it is.

Not to rip out too much from scripture, but the Sun is its own light, and the Moon is its own light. The Moon doesn't reflect anything, which of course, leads to the question, "If the Moon is self-illuminating and it's like this big glowing nightlight, what exactly did we land on?" We landed on some dirty grey surface, and it wasn't glowing as far as I can tell, so no. The Moon and the Sun are their own entities, and they're much smaller and much closer.

Q. So, they are not rotating then?

A. No. But they could be instanced. The Sun, you don't have to do anything with it because it's so bright. Nobody looks at it, and photography is really limited. But with the Moon, whatever it's displaying at, it seems not only is it displaying its own image, but I also believe that there is a structure underneath the Moon. It is what you see it is, but there's something underneath it. We don't know what it is. I believe it's displaying per region, which we've only been able to in the last 15 years or so, to do it with software. Some people say that the Moon is orientated one was, but if you go down to the Southern hemisphere, it's the other way, and that's probably because it's instanced, meaning you can change the Moon's display properties depending on where you are.

Instanced – is a way of executing the same drawing commands many times in a row, with each producing a slightly different result. This can be a very efficient method of rendering a large amount of geometry with very few API calls.[8]

Q. Now we go to curvature. So, when you are out at sea, on a ship, and you look at another ship on the horizon, the lower part of the boat is obscured due to the curvature of the Earth. How do you explain that?

A. I would have been right there with you a few years ago. There's no way I'm going to convince the listener in a short show. The curvature is a perfect question because we all know the boats drop off in the distance, right?

Well, we thought that until the new HD cameras came out. What we were really watching was you watch a boat with your naked eye, and you go out to a certain distance, and it seems like it's gone. Then, you take your HD camera, and you zoom in, and there's the ship again. So, you leave and don't zoom in all the way, and the ship will disappear again. You crank up the zoom, and the ship comes back. You can do this almost infinitely until the atmosphere starts distorting it.

The point is once it gets out to a certain distance, it shouldn't be viewable anymore. The curve is eight inches per mile square, not eight inches times every mile. It is eight inches times every mile times itself. So, when a boat gets out to a certain distance, you shouldn't be able to see it. When it gets out 15 miles, it should be hundreds of feet below the Earth.

We see it with solid structures all the time. Look up online timelapse of Chicago from the other side of the lake. That's 52 miles, almost 1700 feet, yet here's a full 18-hour time-lapse of the Chicago skyline. People in mainstream media say that's it's a mirage. Really, what's the time-lapse doing? That's 18 hours of mirage. The camera is stationary, and it goes into nighttime. Plus, there are several weather conditions. The thing never blurs. It doesn't go inverted. The Chicago skyline is right there, 52 miles. You should not be able to see it.

Q. How do you tackle the compass? The North and South Pole.

A. A question of, "How far do you have to go before the South Pole takes over the needle on the compass?" It never flips. It's always the North that carries it. One thing you've got to look at is, does magnetic north move? Yes, it does. Does that mean it's the stationary North Pole? If this thing is all mechanical, what I mean by that is we're basically living in a Hollywood backlot machine, then the magnetic force, what is gravity, and what is magnetism, is also part of a mechanical system that is underneath you.

As far as what happens down in the south, we don't know. We are still working on it.

We can tell you it's not what everyone in mainstream science is advertising.

Q. When was it first realized by humans that we were not on a round planet?

A. I think the secret societies, again. Take your pick on which ones, but they knew for a long time. But until you have the technology to exploit it, what do you do with that information? Let's say that you are the King of France in the year 1500, and you have a true map of the world. What do you do with that information? Because you've got wooden ships and balloons to carry people, so, what do you do with it? You don't do anything.

They didn't even know for sure. That's why Admiral Bird was looking for it from 1927 or 28, all the way until his death in 1957. That's what he was looking for. So, they weren't even sure, and I think they almost gave up in 1954 when they let him go on television and say "that Antarctica is made out of money. So, let's go and make some money."

Q. How about the seasons? How do they work?

A. The Sun and the Moon do not take the same path, like a record needle on a record. As the song progresses, it goes further into the record. That's what the Sun and the Moon's path do. They don't travel in the exact same circle or path every time. Sometimes they travel further out at a wider radius. Sometimes they zoom in closer to the North Pole. You combine that with all the other systems, again, purely mechanical. The jet stream above, the underwater conveyor system, tinker with those a few notches, and there are your seasons.

Q. Where do you think this is all going?

A. I think some form of disclosure. The mass media didn't have to cover it. Nothing in the mass media happens by accident. There's some ulterior motive here. It seems to be part of a bigger revelation, and we're still trying to figure out what that is.

So, we think the Flat Earth is going to be falsely discovered, and then that will be part of something bigger. The builders of this place wanted us to figure it out eventually, but it was delayed somewhat. I believe it was supposed to be discovered in the 1970s by maybe a private exploration team, a private rocket company, but that was delayed because the "powers that be" figured it out and had the ability to cover it up for a long time.

I think it's like the "one hundred monkey effect," where when enough people figure it out, it'll sound the alarm, and the builders show up.

Q. What do you say to the people that claim to have been abducted by aliens?

A. I think there very well could be people that were abducted by aliens, but I don't think those aliens were from other planets. This "enclosed world model" changes everything from that standpoint. There is no Solar System. There is no Universe with billions and billions of light-years and things that are far away and distances that just don't make sense. It's all way more efficient and way more compact.

Are there spaceships flying around out there? You bet there are. I've watched them on night vision many times for years. Get some night vision binoculars, go outside yourself, and the sky just lights up. It's like a traffic jam sometimes. You think they're satellites until you see them do some weird ballistic movements that you'd never see in a satellite.

I don't think that we were the first civilization to live here. I think there were others before us, and there are survivors of those civilizations. And they have rules to follow. They could be in here with us. They could be in other enclosed worlds just on the outside of this place.

Listen to the full interview with Mark Sargent on my website:

www.alanrwarren.com/hom-
podcast-
episodes/episode/b466427d/flat-
earth-society-mark-sargent-
flahback

Interview Afterthoughts

This was the first subject that I wanted to cover in this conspiracy interview book because I think it speaks to the core of one of the biggest issues we all face in the 21st century – the lack of an education in science.

The human race from all countries has relied on science and knowledge from previous generations to achieve success in our current or future problems we are faced with. When one generation figures out how to accomplish something, it is usually written about, and the information is spread throughout the world for anybody to use in their own progress. So, in medicine, when a generation faces the Spanish Flu, doctors discover a cure, usually in a vaccine, and give it to the survivors of the community so that we continue to live healthily. We have seen this process happen several times with many diseases, from polio, smallpox, to measles.

In Astronomy, we learned where Earth's place was in our galaxy and about the Sun, Moon, stars, and other planets around us. We made progress in flying into space and landing on the Moon. We set up a space station and launched several satellites in our planet's orbit to achieve the great communications we have today. I could go on forever with our history of achieving things from our previous generation's knowledge in every subject imaginable.

So, why is this now being ignored by so many in the current generations? From the interviews I have done, many of our guests question some of the collective principle knowledge bases.

It seems to come from a lack of trust in our government. It always comes down to the government being behind the large scheme to fool the common people in the world for some sinister reason. Or a group of humans gets labeled as wanting to control the world – the Jewish community seems to get that one the most. Some blame a group of elite wealthy people, the Illuminati, for being in complete control of everything that happens. Quite often, the wealthy liberals of the country or Hollywood members are put into that group. Then, there's the straightforward "blame it on Satan." The Christians of the world who put their faith in God or Jesus blame everything awful on Satan. I don't think they realize that in order to believe in Satan, you have to be a Christian.

This last group seems to be what the Flat-Earthers fall in to. Often in this interview, our guest drew on scriptures and old beliefs from the Christian Bible. It was a common belief among Christians before the 19th century that the world was flat. Sargent claims that the major countries of the world got together to create a pact that nobody goes to Antarctica for the reason they didn't want anybody to discover that it was the edge of the Flat Earth. That's interesting, considering that there are more than 200 substations set up in Antarctica by different scientific teams from around the world.

He also claims that there was no space race, but in actuality, America and Russia were sending rockets in the air to see how far it was before they would hit the ceiling of the dome that surrounded us. This certainly plays into the "Fake Moon-landing theory" but falls short when we use satellites to talk to each other, send photos in a matter of seconds, or watch TV.

To think that all of the officers and scientists that have ever worked on any of the space programs in the last 50 years for NASA, Russia, China, or any other country were in on this is even crazier.

Flat-Earthers believe that every picture of film from outer space has been created to help get us to believe the world is round and that even the pilots are lying to us. How many pilots do you know personally? I know a few, and they laugh at such things. These conspiracy theorists go out and attack astronauts like Buzz Aldrin by accusing their whole lives of being a lie. It links back to a major distrust of not only our government or rich elites but also people that are our neighbors. It seems that all it takes to be distrusted is for you to be a supporter of government and science.

Throughout the whole two-hour interview, Sargent only had theories that he developed from his feelings, not science or any hard evidence. He showed nothing but the paranoia of anything in the mainstream. Nothing is real here, but God will fix everything one day.

---

1. Modern flat Earth beliefs - Wikipedia. https://en. wikipedia.org/wiki/Modern_flat_Earth_beliefs
2. Copernican heliocentrism - Wikipedia. https://en. wikipedia.org/wiki/Copernican_heliocentrism
3. Antarctic Treaty System - SCAR. https://scar.org/policy/ antarctic-treaty-system/
4. Why Aren't The Van Allen Belts A Barrier To Spaceflight?. https://www.forbes.com/sites/jillianscudder/2017/06/ 16/astroquizzical-van-allen-belts-barrier-spaceflight/
5. Aerospace Legacy Engineering and Technology Recovery .... http://aletro.org/aletro%20bios%2012_2_13.pdf
6. Capricorn One (1978) - Rotten Tomatoes. https://www. rottentomatoes.com/m/capricorn_one
7. Neil Armstrong - Wikipedia. https://en.wikipedia.org/ wiki/Neil_Armstrong
8. Instanced Rendering | Drawing with OpenGL | InformIT. https://www.informit.com/articles/article.aspx?p= 2033340&seqNum=5

We've Never Been to the Moon

The Conspiracy Theory

During the interview with the last guest, Mark Sargent, about the Flat Earth Theory, we heard a lot about the Moon. It seems that Flat-Earthers don't believe there is even a Moon as we know it, or how it's portrayed on movies and media, and that we have never been there.

So, to look further into this, I found a few people that covered the Fake Moon Landing Conspiracy Theory in detail. And we found Marcus Allen in the UK.

Marcus Allen is the UK publisher of *Nexus Magazine,* which he introduced to the UK in 1994. *Nexus* is the world's leading alternative news magazine, covering health, future science, hidden history, the unexplained, and UFOs. *Nexus* originates from Australia and is now sold in over 100 countries, including the USA and Canada. Marcus pursues his lifelong interest in the unexplained on a full-time basis. The Moon Landings is just one of the many "taboo" subjects he has investigated, around which new questions have been raised that have yet to be satisfactorily answered. Marcus has appeared on many TV shows during the past 20 years to discuss the Apollo Moon Landing controversy: BBC TV, Channel 4, Channel 5, Sky News, Sci-Fi and Discovery Channels, Edge Media, as well as being interviewed on numerous national and local radio shows in the UK and the USA. He has also given many public presentations throughout Britain and Europe, and one in Kathmandu, Nepal, which directly challenges the "official" story of men landing on the Moon over 50 years ago.[1]

Interview with Marcus Allen

In February of 2017, we did a two-hour interview with him.

Q. One of the things that you have written about in *Nexus Magazine* is the Moon landing of the Apollo, which we all saw on television back on July 20, 1969. But you claim that it didn't happen the way we think it did. What got you into researching that event?

A. That's a good way of putting it. I'm old enough to have been up at 3:30 in the morning on July 20, 1969, which was what time it was in London when they landed. I watched them jumping around on my black and white TV like everyone else. For 25 years after that, I believed in what I've been told. I had no reason not to believe what I've been told. That man landed on the Moon and returned safely to the Earth.

Nearly 50 years later, I don't have that view anymore. Man has not landed on the Moon and never had to return safely to the Earth because he never left it. What started the whole process was when I was at a lecture given by an American in Glastonbury in 1992. He was talking about something completely different, but he had happened to mention almost in passing, "Oh, there's Moon landing pictures. They weren't taken on the Moon. They were all fabricated here on Earth." I thought, what are you talking about? That's complete nonsense. He's obviously been affected by something in America, but I'll check it out.

Now, I attended photographic college and was trained as a photographer in London. It was a very interesting career as a photographer in London in the 1960s. I was trained technically how to develop film, how to use film, how to use studios, how to use cameras. I knew about film. In the early 1990s, I decided I would check out those pictures he was talking about, but I had to find them. We didn't have the internet in those days, so I had to go to an astronomy show to buy a set of photographs of the Apollo Moon landing, which I did.

So, I started to look at them and thought, "I see what he means. They don't appear to be taken under the conditions that we are told exist on the Moon. They appear to be taken under conditions which would be a studio set up, or controlled environment on Earth." The more I looked at them, the more I started examining how they were taken.

They were using Hasselblad cameras, which are very good cameras. I've had to use Hasselblad cameras. I know they are quite different to use, and they have excellent lenses. They produce very good pictures. I thought if it's such a good camera, how did they use it to get such good pictures on the Moon. Then I found out that they didn't have a viewfinder in the camera. That's not a major problem because you can take quite good pictures without a viewfinder, but you have to take lots and lots to make sure you get them generally pointing in the right direction. I also understood about bracketing, which is taking the same picture with different exposures to make sure that you get the correct exposure. That hadn't been done. That's when I realized that there were major problems here.

That led me to start looking into the other aspects of Apollo, as the rockets. Were they powerful enough to do what we were told they did? How did they get back? The re-entry, I'm told, occurred at 25,000 miles an hour when they hit the atmosphere. Were the heat shields strong enough to protect them?

I started getting into the technicalities of the Apollo, and the more I looked at it, the more evident it became that not everything was as it seemed. There appeared to be a major problem with getting men to the Moon.

The major problem is basically the radiation, which we know exists around Earth – the Van Allen Radiation Belts. They've been known to exist for many years. They probably existed since the planet was created four and a half billion years ago. They are created by the Earth's magnetic field, and they protect the Earth from the Solar particle events generated by the Sun and the Galactic Cosmic Rays generated in deep space, which we know exists. There are no two ways about it.

One of the problems is protecting humans. Now, on Earth, we are protected, not only by the Van Allen Belt but the atmosphere surrounding the Earth. There are about 60 miles of atmosphere above our head. That's why atmospheric pressure is 14.7 pounds per square inch. That is the weight of air above your head. Now, if you take that away when you travel above the atmosphere, you get to the vacuum of space where there is no pressure. If you didn't have your own spacesuit with you, you would soon die because the gasses dissolved in your blood would expand, and you'll go pop. These spacesuits work quite well. They are used on the International Space Station, and they were used by the Apollo astronauts to go to the Moon. They obviously protected them from the radiation they had to pass through. It takes about two hours to pass through the radiation belts.

So, I thought if these spacesuits are so good and they protected the astronauts from the radiation, surely these same suits can be used for technicians to go to Chernobyl, Three Mile Island, or Fukushima and clean up the mess.

Radiation is radiation, gamma rays, and X-rays. So, I contacted the manufacturers of the spacesuits, Hamilton Standard in Connecticut, and asked them if these spacesuits could be used to clear up nuclear reactors, and they said no. When I asked them why they said there was no radiation protection built into them. So, I wrote to NASA and asked them if they could be used. I'm still waiting for a reply.

So, the question arises how the astronauts were protected from the radiation and, more importantly, how was the photographic film protected from the radiation. Some of your older listeners will probably remember that when you used to go through airport security following the D.B. Cooper case in the 70s, they introduced X-rays to make sure people weren't carrying bombs onto the planes.

The X-ray machines were a bit unsophisticated then, and they were quite powerful. If you were carrying a photographic film, which is affected by radiation, it causes a fogging effect in the film. So, you were always advised that if you had film, get it hand-searched rather than passing through the X-ray machine.

So, why wasn't their photographic film affected by it? Because the film or pictures of the Moon that I was looking at all appeared to be unaffected by any radiation damage. There was no radiation damage in any of the pictures I saw.

At the time, there were only a few pictures I could locate, but now I've seen hundreds, if not thousands, of the Apollo photographs because they're all available online. So, that was a mystery that I still haven't solved – how was the photographic film protected from the radiation damage when on the lunar surface, where NASA tells us the pictures were taken?

I claim they were not taken on the lunar surface of the Moon. They were taken during the training and simulation exercises here on Earth. Nothing to do with Area 51; that was a sideshow. There were plenty of sets that were built to simulate what everybody thought the Moon's surface would look like. These were quite open, and there's nothing secret about them. An astronaut would carry out real-time simulations. Apollo was an 8-day mission, and they carried out an 8-day simulation, so everybody knew what to expect.

During the 8-day simulation, they were all filmed, and they were all photographed. There was no secret about that. So, were these photographs and films taken during these simulation exercises? The very ones that were presented to us as evidence of the alleged landing on the lunar surface? I claim they were. If somebody can prove me wrong, then please do so. But nobody in 20 years has managed to.

Q. You have also mentioned reflection or albedo of the Moon and the lighting. Maybe elaborate on that?

A. Albedo means reflectivity – the amount of light reflected off any surface. As a percentage of the amount of light falling onto the surface, a mirror would reflect 100 percent of the light falling onto it. Black velvet would reflect about 1 percent. It depends on the material onto which the light is falling. It will determine the amount of light reflecting off the material.

The lunar surface, obviously, you can see it at night. You can see it during the day sometimes, as well, if you know where to look. That is reflecting sunlight. The amount of light that falls onto the lunar surface is 100 percent. The amount of light reflected from the lunar surface is 7 percent – a relatively small amount. That's why you can look at the Full Moon at night quite comfortably. You can look at it through a telescope quite comfortably because the amount of light reflecting off the lunar surface is relatively small. You can't look at the Sun though through a telescope unless you want to go blind because it will damage your eyes. We use filters to take a photograph of it.

The Moon reflects 7 percent of the light falling onto it. Now that is the same amount of light that would be reflected off a road surface. The amount of light off the tarmac is about 7 percent, or thereabouts, of the amount of light hitting it.

In photography, you are using light all the time. If the subject that you are trying to photograph does not have sufficient light on it, the film won't record it.

The International Standard Organization (ISO), or speed of the film, is a way of standardizing the sensitivity of any photographic film. You have fast films, and you have slow films. You have all different types of film. The kind of film used on the lunar surface was Kodak Ektachrome film. It's a transparency material, otherwise known as a reversal film. So, you can stick it in a projector and project that image onto a screen. It's the same way that movie films are projected. If you've got a photographic film with a relatively fast speed, Kodak Ektachrome film is rated at 160 ASA, which is a medium-fast film.

The problem with film is unless you have sufficient light falling onto the film through the camera lens, it will not record an image. It cannot do so. Either you let more light onto the film, or you decrease the shutter speed, so it takes longer to open the shutter, say from a 120th of a second to a 60th of a second. You can adjust the amount of light falling onto the film.

But on the lunar surface, you've got a very strange situation. The lunar surface is illuminated by the Sun, the only source of illumination. Yet, in several of the pictures I was looking at, it appeared that there was illumination onto the object. In this case, it was the astronaut climbing down the ladder of the lunar lander. He's in the shadow of the lander because you can see where the Sun is. It's behind the lander. But he appears in quite well-illuminated condition. So, where did that light come from?

We know that no flash-films were carried, and no reflectors were carried. People will say that it's the reflection of the lunar surface. But any photographer will tell you that you do not use a road surface as a reflector. It doesn't reflect enough light into the subject, especially if the subject is vertical to the reflector. In this case, the surface of the Moon.

So, that was the first key point that there was something seriously wrong with the photographs. They appear to have been professionally produced. The only place that you can professionally produce photographs is here on Earth.

That's where I claim the photographs were taken, here on Earth and not on the lunar surface.

Q. They must have known what they were going to be faced with when they got to the Moon. Why would NASA not take any additional lighting with them?

A. That's a good question. I don't know why they didn't. There are certainly images that have been produced by NASA on the Apollo 11 specifically, where trained scientists have looked at the photographs and calculated the actual position of the flashgun that illuminated it. You can tell by the highlights of light that appear on the astronaut's heel on his boot. But they didn't carry any. I've read all the press releases. I've read all the information about all of the Apollo missions. Not one of them ever mentioned an additional lighting source was carried. They had torches that they used inside the spacecraft.

There were no electronic flashguns. There were no portable reflectors other than the astronauts themselves. They wore basically a white spacesuit. The point about that is, yes, it will reflect light, but not a sufficient amount of light to produce the illustrations that we saw. A company has produced a rather strange video claiming they had proven Armstrong's spacesuit was sufficient to reflect enough light to produce the appearance of a reflector. It's absolute rubbish.

NVIDIA recently decided to debunk this particular argument in order to show off the power of its latest graphics technologies. With a great deal of effort, they completely recreated every element of the moon landing scene as a 3D model and then added the Sun as the sole light source. It turns out that's Neil Armstrong standing there taking pictures with one of the Hasselblad cameras still on the moon. The spacesuit that Armstrong was wearing actually served as a light source. The white, Teflon-coated suits were almost mirror-like in their reflectiveness, causing them to act as light sources in the scene. Once the spacesuit light source was accounted for, the computer light rendering became virtually identical to the original photograph of Aldrin.

Another popular argument is that since the moon photos don't show any stars, they must have been faked. This is simply a lack of understanding of how exposures work. NVIDIA also did simulations showing what the scene would have to look like for stars.[2]

They used all the wrong figures. They used the wrong percentage of light reflected off those materials, which you could calculate quite easily. It was yet another attempt to try and dissuade the people from believing that nobody has landed on the Moon.

Q. What about the evidence that they brought back with them? Such as samples, Moon rocks, and air samples. I'm sure that they took readings when they were there too.

A. We're told they brought back 340 kilos of Moon rock over the six missions that landed. One of them didn't land, Apollo 13. Yes, so 340 kilos of Moonrock. Have you seen any recently?

Q. Well, it's not like I have a key chain or anything like that.

A. Here in London, we have the famous Science Museum, and in the Science Museum, there is an exhibition on space travel. They show the Apollo 10 lunar lander, which was never used for landing. It was used for the Apollo 10 command module.

Alongside it, there is a display case with Moonrock written on it. There's a tiny little sliver of something which the scientists say is Moonrock, so it must be. If you go to any museum in the United States, they display Moonrock. But a lot of them have lost the Moonrock.

There was a famous case a few years back of the Dutch Moonrock. It was displayed in the Rijksmuseum, which is the national museum of Holland in Amsterdam. It's definitely worth a visit. In that museum, there was a display of Moonrock. A few years ago, the Rijksmuseum was undergoing renovations, so they had to remove some of these displays. One of the displays that were removed was the Moonrock display. So, geologists in Holland decided to take the opportunity to examine them.

It was petrified wood. If you want to check it out, just put Dutch Moonrock into Google, and you'll get the pictures of it. It was something about two or three inches long. It was black, and it was displayed as a Moon rock presented to the Dutch Prime Minister in 1969 by Armstrong, Aldrin, and Collins.

So, one would tend to believe that this was a piece of rock brought back from the Moon. It wasn't. There's no petrified wood on the Moon. Either somebody nicked it and put it on eBay to get some money, or it was just fake in the first place. It was not a piece of Moonrock. Now, that's just one example.

The Dutch national museum said that one of its prized possessions, a Moon rock supposedly brought back from the Moon by U.S. astronauts from the Apollo 11, is just a piece of petrified wood. The museum acquired the rock after the death of former Prime Minister Willem Drees in 1988. Drees received it as a private gift on Oct. 9, 1969, from then-U.S. ambassador J. William Middendorf during a visit by the three Apollo 11 astronauts, part of their "Giant Leap" goodwill tour after the first moon landing.

Apparently, no one thought to doubt it since it came from the Prime Minister's collection. One important unanswered question is why Drees was given the stone. He was 83-years old in 1969 and had been out of office for 11 years.

The space agency told the museum then that it was possible the Netherlands had received a rock. NASA gave Moonrocks to more than 100 countries in the early 1970s, but those were from later missions. In 2006, a space expert informed the museum it was unlikely NASA would have given away any Moon rocks three months after Apollo returned to Earth.[3]

Q. So, you are saying that there is no Moonrock here on Earth? I've seen it in other museums.

A. How do you know it's Moon rock? Just because it says it is. But there is genuine Moon rock here on Earth. It was recovered by the Russians on an unmanned craft, Luna 1 and Luna 2. They were able to land the craft on the Moon and grab a few grams, 300 grams in total of lunar soil, the dusty stuff on the surface.

The Russians were remarkably able to remotely control landers and spacecraft coming back to Earth. Now, when the Russians landed with a few hundred grams, 300 grams is a little short of 1 pound in weight, so it's not a great deal as compared to the Americans who had about 800 pounds.

So, you've got an imbalance here. The Russians are quite generous when it comes to sharing their scientific achievement. They were quite willing to exchange with NASA samples of the Moonrock, which they had allegedly recovered, and exchange it with the Russian samples. NASA refused. It took a lot of very high political pressure to get

NASA to agree to exchange a few grams sample, two years later, of their Moonrock. It's obvious they had something to hide.

The Soviet Union attempted but failed to make crewed lunar landings in the 1970s, but they succeeded in landing three robotic Luna spacecraft with the capability to collect and return small samples to Earth. A combined total of less than half-a-kilogram of the material was returned. In 1993, three small rock fragments from Luna 16, weighing 200 mg, were sold for $442,500 USD at Sotheby's. In 2018, the same three Luna 16 rock fragments sold for $855,000 USD at Sotheby's:

- Luna 16 – 101 g (3.6 oz) in 1970
- Luna 20 – 30 g (1.1 oz) in 1972
- Luna 24 – 170 g (6.0 oz) in 1976[4]

Now that Russia can access information about Apollo in an unrestricted way, they've decided to investigate it. One of the investigations was done by using a very accurate 16 mm. copy of the Saturn V rocket taking off. The first thing they had to establish was the speed at which the film was shot, in this case, 24 frames per second. That would allow you to do measurements of time and distance because the film is a 3-minute continuous sequence from take off to when the Saturn V rocket disappears.

Long story short, the Saturn V rocket was not moving fast enough to achieve the speed necessary to put into lunar orbit the 46 tons of we're told, as it did. They can calculate the speed the Saturn V rocket was moving at by looking at the frames in this particular film. It's been done in great detail. The appearance is that the Saturn V rocket was nowhere near powerful enough to achieve the escape velocity required to subsequently achieve lunar orbit, which is 25,000 miles an hour.

If the Saturn V rocket wasn't powerful enough, why was it necessary to say it was? Why was it necessary to say that it occurred the way it did when it can be deconstructed and has been deconstructed by pretty eminent scientists that know what they're doing?

Saturn V was an American super heavy-lift launch vehicle certified for human-rating used by NASA between 1967 and 1973. It consisted of three stages, each fueled by liquid propellants. It was developed to support the Apollo program for human exploration of the Moon and was later used to launch Skylab, the first American space station. The Saturn V was launched 13 times from Kennedy Space Center with no loss of crew or payload.[5]

If any of your listeners are interested in seeing that particular sequence and the calculations made to establish that it couldn't produce the power, the website is *aulis.com*. There are many articles there by Russian scientists and filmmakers deconstructing much of the Apollo story.

Q. Now, you also talk about Apollo 13. What have you discovered about it?

A. Apollo 13 was launched on April 11, 1970. We are told that it was halfway to the Moon when an oxygen tank exploded. They had to get back to Earth and jerry-rig the oxygen and carbon dioxide scrubbers so that they could survive the journey back. They got back and were big heroes. Tom Hanks made a wonderful film about it. That's the official story of Apollo 13.

But how many people are familiar with the fact that on April 12th, one day after the launch of the Saturn V rocket carrying the three Apollo 13 astronauts, a Russian submarine in the Bay of Biscay recovered an Apollo command capsule, which, according to the report, had fallen from the sky and transferred to a fishing boat because the submarine couldn't fit it inside.

The Apollo command module was taken by this Russian fishing boat, which is in effect a Russian spy ship. It eventually reached Murmansk, which is in Northern Russia and next to Norway. On September the 4th,

1970, an American coast guard vessel, the Southwind, arrived at Murmansk on a goodwill mission, which is strange because it was the first American coast guard vessel ever to have reached Murmansk on any sort of mission, goodwill or otherwise.

The Apollo command module was handed over by the Russians to be loaded onto the Southwind, the U.S. coast guard ship, which had quite coincidently had its fore-gun removed. Usually, a coast guard cutter will have a 4-inch gun on its front deck. In order to accommodate the command module and its return to the United States, the gun had been removed a few months prior to this particular mission.

The command module was returned to America and is now exhibited in a museum in Kansas. It's a story that is generally not very well known, but it was reported in the American airforce paper *Stars and Stripes* in 1970.

Now, if the day after the official launch of the Apollo 13, the command module can be removed from the Atlantic Ocean by a

Russian submarine, have we been told the real story of the Apollo 13? It appears not. It appears that there is much more to this story than we are led to believe. It requires a whole lot more investigation. For anybody who wants to look at this information, the *Aulis* website carries a few articles from the Russian perspective.

Q. Why didn't the Russians blow the whistle on this early on?

A. That's the question I'm normally asked. Why would they blow the whistle? Now, we have to go back a little bit here to Yuri Gagarin and his famous circling of the Earth, the first man to orbit the Earth, Yuri Gagarin. Prior to that happening, he had obviously made several attempts. You don't just do it the first time out.

There were two Italian brothers, one of them is still alive, that could hear the Russian spacecraft when they passed over Italy on their way orbiting the Earth. They were Ham radio operators, and they would listen in. They would hear several Russian cosmonauts who were in serious trouble in their space crafts.

The point of the story is that there were many unfortunate events in the Russian space program where cosmonauts could not return from orbit because of their retro-rockets. This is how the Russians returned to Earth. Either they didn't work, or work sufficiently enough to be able to slow the craft down in order to land. There was one story of the craft burning up while trying to re-enter the atmosphere. The re-entry into the Earth's atmosphere causes extreme heat on the spacecraft, and transmissions appear to indicate that the cosmonaut was dying through heat.

So, the Russians didn't blow the whistle on the Americans because they knew perfectly well that if they did, the Americans would just go and blow the whistle on the Russians. They would show that the Russians didn't do half the things they said they were going to do.

Possibly the real reason the Russians didn't blow the whistle was that they didn't need to. They knew perfectly well that much of the Apollo program was faked because they were aware of the dangers themselves. They tried to land on the Moon as well.

At the time of Apollo 11, there was a launch by the Russians of another unmanned lunar craft that was going to try and land on the Moon before the Americans did. Yes, there was a space race, but the Russians were not stupid enough to try and launch somebody into almost certain death from radiation. They were asked when they were going to try and land a man on the Moon, and their answer was straightforward, "when we can return him safely due to the dangers of radiation." They knew it was virtually impossible to get through it.

Happening at the same time as Apollo 11 was something even more important for Russia. Russia is a relatively small economy even today. It's about the size of Italy. But it has one major export, and that is natural gas. The gas has to be transported from Siberia into Europe. Thirty percent of

European gas consumption comes from Russia. In September 1968, Russia signed the first contracts to supply natural gas into western Europe. Because so much depended on the supply of natural gas, their economy was dependent on their natural gas. They were not about to jeopardize this extremely important conference where these contracts would be signed. As far as they were concerned, space was a bit of a sideshow.

Q. Okay, so, if I were to accept everything that you have said up until now, that the Apollo Moon landing was faked, I have to ask, have we gone to the Moon since then?

A. Well, there are unconfirmed indicators that we have been on the Moon since. This is the secret space program, the X-37B, that we know exists. It's a smaller version of the space shuttle that goes on nine or 18-month missions. That's long enough to get to Mars and back.

What is this X-37B that NASA isn't telling us? There are various other space crafts that do exist. The X-37B certainly does exist, and it's been on extremely long missions, but nobody knows what those missions are or where it's been to.

The Boeing X-37, also known as the Orbital Test Vehicle, is a reusable robotic spacecraft. It is boosted into space by a launch vehicle, then re-enters Earth's atmosphere and lands as a spaceplane. The X-37 is operated by the United States Space Force and was previously operated by Air Force Space Command until 2019 for orbital spaceflight missions intended to demonstrate reusable space technologies. The X-37B is a modified version of the NASA X-37A, built for the U.S. Air Force. Two were built and have been used for multiple orbital missions.

X-37B

General characteristics:

- Crew: none
- Length: 29 ft 3 in
- Wingspan: 14 ft 11 in
- Height: 9 ft 6 in

- Max takeoff weight: 11,000 lb.
- Electrical power: Gallium arsenide solar cells with lithium-ion batteries
- Payload bay: 7 × 4 ft
- Orbital speed: 17,426 mph
- Orbit: Low Earth orbit
- Orbital time: 270 days[6]

It's possible that somebody has been to the Moon. But if so, why is NASA spending so much time and effort putting together the Orion capsule, which was first flown unmanned in December 2014 and will next fly at the end of next year. That's four years after its first mission and three years before anyone will climb in and fly it. That's the total time that it took for Apollo to occur.

Either there is something highly secret going on, which we will call the secret space program, and this business with radiation was solved years ago. There are fleets of crafts out in space; maybe even Mars has been reached by humans.

As far as ever going to the Moon, I've seen no evidence to indicate that they have. Again, they would need to overcome the dangers of radiation. Humans are extraordinarily innovative creatures, but they are also very delicate. We are designed to live here on Earth with gravity and without radiation. You go to the Moon, you take away gravity, and increase radiation. As for the heat, there's so much of that, so you've got to remove that as well. I haven't seen any information or evidence that we have the ability to travel to the Moon today. We certainly didn't have it in 1969.

Q. So, what was the reason for the Americans to fake the Moon landing? There are lots of stories out there, such as it was because of the Vietnam War.

My Lai Massacre, also called Pinkville Massacre, was the mass killing of as many as 500 unarmed villagers by U.S. soldiers in the hamlet of My Lai on March 16, 1968, during the Vietnam War. William Calley, the second lieutenant, was the only American convicted of his role in the massacre.

A. That's part of it, yes. It was a distraction. Don't forget the My Lai Massacre in Vietnam. In the summer of 1968 in Vietnam, there was a real unpleasant massacre of 500 people in My Lai, Vietnam. Vietnam was getting extremely unpleasant. Americans were dying in the hundreds every day. It was on television, and people were becoming extremely angry about the whole Vietnam war.

There was also the economic problems that were going on at the time. There was the Cold War with the Russians. It was necessary to introduce some form of distraction – a Disneyfication. I'm not saying that Disney had anything to do with it, but he was most likely of a character to have assisted NASA in their fantasy, which was basically what the Moon landings were.

The Apollo 11 astronauts were heroes. They appeared on the covers of magazines.

Even today, Buzz Aldrin is revered. Nobody would ever challenge him or question him.

Bart Sibrel was rude to Aldrin. He called him a coward and a liar, which is why he got punched. To be fair to Bart, he has agreed that he went much too far, and he has apologized to Buzz Aldrin as a result. I think there is a degree of truce between them. But why wouldn't he swear on a Bible that he had walked on the lunar surface? That's all he's been asked to do. If you had walked on the lunar surface and if you were of a religious persuasion, you'd say, "Give me the Bible. How many have you got? I'll swear on as many as you like."

Bart Sibrel is an American conspiracy theorist who has written, produced and directed works in support of the false belief that the Apollo Moon landings between 1969 and 1972 were staged by NASA under the control of the CIA. In his film *A Funny Thing Happened on the Way to the Moon,* Sibrel asked that various Apollo astronauts put their hand on the Bible and swear an oath that they walked on the moon. In the case of the Apollo 11 astronaut Buzz Aldrin, whom Sibrel arranged to meet on a false pretense outside the Luxe Hotel in Beverly Hills, the interaction resulted in Aldrin punching Sibrel and in significant publicity, but no criminal charges.[7]

He wouldn't do it. And Neil Armstrong wouldn't do it. Even when he was offered $5,000 for a charity of his choice, he wouldn't swear on a Bible that he had walked on the lunar surface. Why not? When Michael Collins, who didn't walk on the Moon as he was in the command module on Apollo 11, was asked, he went and punched the cameraman.

A few of the astronauts have sworn on the Bible that was offered to them. But the general approach of astronauts is of people who are under extreme psychological pressure, and I have a great deal of sympathy for them because all of the astronauts were military men.

Our government would never lie to use, right? NASA would never tell us a lie either, right?

Q. Then there's the question of how many people would have to be involved in such a cover-up, and how they could keep it secret for so long?

A. That's a very good point and is one that comes up a lot when I'm giving a presentation. One hundred thousand people worked for the Apollo program during the 1960s. Now, these were people employed by the many contracting companies such as Boeing, Lockheed Martin, and many other companies. They were doing the very best job they could. They had bought into President John F. Kennedy's amazing speech in May of 1961 that they were going to land on the Moon before the decade is out.

But at that time, no American, except Alan Shepard had ever been into space, and Shepard had only gone up and back down again. Nobody knew if they could do it, and this was called a presidential challenge. We all know what happened to Kennedy. He was killed two and a half years later. It became incumbent on the American industry to rally around and to fulfill their martyred President's challenge.

They were building the best rockets they could. They were under the direction of Wernher von Braun, who was brought into America from Germany after the war from Operation Paperclip. Under that operation, Braun and other Nazis were considered the not real bad Nazis because they had rocket knowledge.

By the way, these 100,000 people were also the gardeners, security staff, cleaners, doorkeepers, cafeteria workers, and all the people who were employed in a large corporation to keep it running. Obviously, there were scientists, and engineers or technologists, who were the people that were hands-on making rockets, making landers, making control centers, and making spacesuits. These were people doing the very best job they could.

They had no need to know. Are you seriously saying that the people in Boeing knew what the people making the spacesuits knew? No, of course not. Were the people in California working at Lockheed know what the people in Huntsville were doing? No, they did not.

This was also a matter of National Security. When National Security is involved in America, I understand one of the things that are introduced is compartmentalization. You know enough to do your own job and nothing more because you don't need to know.

Maybe 30, 40, or 50 tops people would have had a knowledge that not everything was as good as we were being told. Obviously, the astronauts were involved. The senior staff at NASA would have been involved.

At some point, probably before the fire in Apollo 1 in January 1967, or before, that it was becoming obvious getting to the Moon was actually a very seriously difficult problem and was highly unlikely to be achieved within the next three years. So, Plan B was put into effect. Plan B was the creation of the fantasy of landing on the Moon. By filming all the training and simulation exercises, who would know the difference? Because nobody has been to the Moon.

Apollo 1, initially designated AS-204, was the first crewed mission of the United States Apollo program, the undertaking to land the first humans on the Moon. It was planned to launch on February 21, 1967, as the first low Earth orbital test of the Apollo command and service module. The mission never flew; a cabin fire during a launch rehearsal test at Cape Kennedy Air Force Station Launch Complex 34 on January 27 killed all three crew members Command Pilot Virgil "Gus" Grissom, Senior Pilot Ed White, and Pilot Roger B. Chaffee and destroyed the command module. The name Apollo 1, chosen by the crew, was made official by NASA in their honor after the fire.[8]

If the people involved, the film crews who were filming it, were NASA employees, then they only needed to know that they were photographing the training exercises. So, the astronauts could be debriefed, "say don't put your foot there you'll fall over," or "Do a little bit more over there." That's all the debrief would need to be. They had no idea the film was going to be used for any other purpose.

The photographic film was used to produce the photographs, copies of which I bought over 20 years ago. Many of which are now on the internet and examined quite closely if you want to. The originals of those photographs, which are transparencies, are held in an air-conditioned controlled booth in Houston. Nobody has ever seen them since they were put there. Despite what apologists for NASA would say, they are called PANS, by the way, Pro Apollo Nutters, who will support NASA in spite of any evidence to the contrary.

As for the telemetry of the Apollo 11, that's all gone completely – completely disappeared, and nobody knows where it is. Why not? It's one of the seminal events in American history, and the evidence for it has vanished.

The Apollo 11 missing tapes were those that were recorded from Apollo 11's slow-scan television (SSTV) telecast in its raw format on telemetry data tape at the time of the first Moon landing in 1969 and subsequently lost. The data tapes were used to record all transmitted data (video as well as telemetry) for backup. At the time, the NTSC broadcast was recorded on many videotapes and kinescope films. Many of these low-quality recordings remain intact. In the early 1980s, NASA's Landsat program was facing a severe data tape shortage, and it is likely the tapes were erased and reused at this time.[9]

Q. So, what is the future of space travel for us?

A. They are claiming that they want to get humans to Mars. Unless they come up with some seriously different method of protecting humans, they'll never get to Mars.

Q. Certainly we have that today?

A. Not to get humans to Mars. We've got the rockets to launch, yes. We have the facilities to get there, despite that famous film *The Martian* with Matt Damon, a great piece of film making that was all based on the fact that NASA did a great deal to check out all the details and had very good facts about Mars. But it's about protecting humans because they never discussed or mentioned the problems of radiation. That was one of the things that were missing from the film.

In the film *Interstellar*, which is about space travel and NASA supports as well because NASA likes to support films which are well made to do with space travel, there's a comment in the film made by the lead character, Matthew McConaughey, where he's talking to his daughter's schoolteacher and discussing the Apollo mission. This film is set in the future. The schoolteacher says that the books are being changed to reflect the fact that Apollo was a brilliantly executed propaganda exercise to ensure that the Soviet Union was bankrupted by building useless machines.

One of the ways that truth gets out is fictional films, where they introduce a subject that can be considered relevant. The original film about this whole process was *Capricorn One*, which was basically a mission to Mars which failed.

Q. So, what about the private industry of space travel?

A. That's more likely where we will see the next major development. We have Space X, Blue Origin, and we have Virgin. But they are only going into low Earth orbit. None of them are even talking about going much further.

I know Elon Musk says he wants to go to Mars, but that's a brilliant way to promote his company. Nobody has actually asked him how he's going to get there. Getting into lower Earth orbit isn't really a problem, or coming back from low orbit Earth isn't a problem either.

It's coming back from the Moon; that's the real problem. It's called re-entry when you re-enter the Earth's atmosphere at the same speed that you leave, 25,000 miles an hour. The Orion craft, which was launched in December 2014, had a heat shield that almost failed. And it wasn't even coming back at the same speed that it would have if it were coming back from the Moon. The heat shield was said to have been completely re-designed because it didn't work. Why don't they just use the one they did in Apollo? Wouldn't that be the simple answer?

If you look at the Orion capsule, the whole of the structure of the Orion capsule is covered in the space shuttle heat shield tiles, as well as the heat shield on the lower end. Why was it necessary to put space shuttle heat shield tiles all over the Orion capsule? That's not what they did on Apollo. Apollo was an aluminum craft with a heat shield on its base that we're told returned from lunar orbit or lunar landing, but the plasma gas that is generated by the heat shield reaches a temperature of 4000 degrees Fahrenheit, which is far in excess of the melting point of aluminum of which the craft was built. It would have melted the damn thing. This is why I say the heat shield on the Apollo did not do what we're told it did.

The whole thing is a fabrication.

Heat Shields – The temperature on the CM's surface climbed up to 5,000 degrees Fahrenheit, but the heat shields protected the inner structure of the CM. The heat shield was ablative, which means that it was designed to melt and erode away from the CM as it heated up. The atmosphere acted like a braking system on the spacecraft. To further slow the CM's descent, the spacecraft used mortar-deployed parachutes. The Apollo spacecraft had three large parachutes and could safely land with only two deployed.[10]

Listen to the full interview with Marcus Allen on my website:

https://shows.acast.com/
houseofmysteryradio/
episodes/marcus-allen-faked-
moon-landing

Interview Afterthoughts

I believe this is one of those things that fit the statement, "A little information can be dangerous." It reminds me of years ago, in the '80s, when I was trying my hand at being a waiter, and some guy that had taken a one-day class on wine came into the restaurant and had to complain about something on every bottle of wine that he ordered. He thought he knew about wine after eight hours of an informal class and used the few terms he still had in his head to impress the lady he was with.

Nexus Magazine has made a living out of trying to define unexplained things in science by applying a motive-based story to explain their theory of NASA not making it to the moon. The unfortunate thing these days is there are a lot of people that haven't been educated very well in the field of science, and they follow this false narrative as being true. They don't have the critical thinking skills to challenge what they hear.

Allen first asserts that because he was a photographer for a magazine back in the 1960s, he understands all the science behind taking photos in space and on the moon. Just saying that out loud makes you shake your head. Then he goes on to try and explain the reflection of the moon. Photography experts not related to NASA have said that the oddities are consistent with what should be expected from a real Moon landing. Allen then claims the film in the cameras would have been fogged by this radiation, but the film was kept in metal containers that stopped radiation from fogging the film's emulsion.

Next, he explains to us that the astronauts could not have survived the trip because of exposure to radiation from the Van Allen radiation belts. The inner belt is the more dangerous one, containing energetic protons. The outer one has less-dangerous low-energy electrons, but the astronauts were shielded from the ionizing radiation by the aluminum hulls of the spacecraft.

Allen is also great at telling us things in a way to make us suspicious of the truth. He easily tells us the story about a museum in Amsterdam that had fake moon landing rocks on display. He craftily suggests that there were no real Moonrocks, and these were all planted by the deep state. But it was just a robbery of the museum in Amsterdam, and the thieves who stole the rocks replaced them with fakes to allow them time to not only get away with the crime but have time to sell them before law enforcement knew they had been stolen and would be looking for them. He forgets to mention that the Apollo program collected 838 pounds of Moonrocks during the six crewed missions. Analyses by scientists worldwide all agree that these rocks came from the Moon, and no published accounts in peer-reviewed scientific journals exist that dispute this claim. The Apollo samples are easily distinguishable from both meteorites and Earth rocks.

Allen's telling of the faked moon landing conspiracy is delivered like an old-time radio theatre broadcast, with rich words and storytelling inflections in his voice that make it easy to get carried away in the story without questioning anything he claims.

After listening, you have to realize that the biggest problem with conspiracy theorists like this is that they only focus on their story. They bring up things that even science hasn't got an explanation for to make you believe in their narrative instead.

Bottom line: The problem with this conspiracy theory is that it carefully forgets to deal with the evidence that we do have about the subject we are talking about. These theorists do this because they don't have anything to counter real science or evidence with, and they know this. So, what better thing to do than to draw the listener's attention away from the truth and focus on the things that can't be explained.

---

1. Marcus Allen | Coast to Coast AM. https://www. coasttocoastam.com/guest/allen-marcus-5650/

2. Neil Armstrong's Spacesuit Served as a Reflector for https://petapixel.com/2014/09/22/neil-armstrongs-spacesuit-served-reflector-bounce-lighting-moon-photos/
3. 'Moon rock' in museum is just petrified wood. https://www.nbcnews.com/id/wbna32581790
4. Moon rock explained. https://everything.explained.today/Moon_rock/
5. Saturn V - Wikipedia. https://en.wikipedia.org/wiki/Saturn_C-5
6. Boeing X-37 - Wikipedia. https://en.wikipedia.org/wiki/Boeing_X-37
7. Capricorn One - WikiMili, The Best Wikipedia Reader. https://wikimili.com/en/Capricorn_One
8. Apollo 1 - Wikipedia. https://en.wikipedia.org/wiki/Apollo_1_disaster
9. Apollo 11 missing tapes - Wikipedia. https://en.wikipedia.org/wiki/Apollo_11_missing_tapes
10. Apollo's Re-entry | HowStuffWorks. https://science.howstuffworks.com/apollo-spacecraft7.htm

Chem Trails & Geoengineering

☙❦❧

The Conspiracy Theory

When I was broadcasting the show out of KFNX in Phoenix, I had unprecedented access to the right-wing conspiracy theorists, probably because KFNX was a well known conservative talk radio station with everyone from Laura Ingraham to Alex Jones. It was a real free-for-all as far as wild stories and lies. I remember back then being told that if you were to drink orange juice from a carton, it would make you gay. There was a special chemical that was used on the inside of these cartons that would make that happen.

Another funny story going around was that somebody, the culprit's names, always changed depending on who I was talking to, who had been spraying us for years with chemicals from American airplanes that were making our shrimp commit suicide. That story always had me trying to figure out in my mind exactly how a shrimp would commit suicide. Would the shrimp be conscious of what it was doing? Was this done by the shrimp jumping onto the shore? Perhaps a protest against being caught and eaten.

Whatever the reason, this chemical poisoning is something I need to find out about. Not only to help those poor shrimps out with their challenges at hand but also to find out if it could be true that someone was spraying us with chemicals. It seemed that the most popular source of such discussion of "chemtrails" was coming from a couple of movies that claimed to be documentaries by Michael Murphy called *What in the World are they Spraying?*, and *Why in the World are they Spraying?*

Interview with Michael Murphy

I found Michael Murphy fairly easy as he was on a promo tour to discuss his movies. He was more than willing to come on the show, not just once but twice. I think he felt safe as I was on a conservative station that liked to promote his type of story.

Not only did he have these two movies out, but he was the "Golden Boy" on Premier Network's *Coast to Coast A.M.* and *Gaia*. Since the passing of the guard from Art Bell, both places have become the go-to locations to get your fix on conspiracies of the wildest kinds.

Michael Murphy claims to have studied Sociology & Anthropology with a Bachelor of Arts at Arizona State University and is the President of Truth Media Productions. As expected, when you go to the Truth Media Productions' Facebook page, its latest posts are claiming that the current pandemic of Corona Virus going on in the world is fake.

Both interviews were recorded in 2015, and these are the highlights. The term "Geoengineering" has become the chemtrail's latest catchword. My guess is that it makes the person claiming this conspiracy theory sound more scientific or credible.

Q. What got you into researching this subject?

A. Noticing that our skies were changing when I lived in Arizona. The skies were deep blue when I moved out to Phoenix from Chicago in 1989, and we would rarely have a blemish in the sky. When I returned back after moving away for a while, I noticed that for about four or five days, we had overcast skies. We had this light haze that almost looked like high cirrus clouds.

So, I began looking into this, and somebody told me about chemtrails and the geoengineering issue, and like most people thought that they were kind of crazy. I began to look more closely and noticed, yes, the airplane trails were turning into this cloud cover that we now had on a regular basis.

I went to a geoengineering conference in San Diego back in 2010. For several days, we listened to geoengineers talk about their plans and proposals to spray 10 to 20 million tons of toxic aluminum and other substances into our skies for what they said was the stated goal of cooling this planet.

That kicked off the film. We released a couple of things via video and brought legitimacy into this chemtrail issue. For the first time, we had the scientific community talking about what they were planning on putting into our sky.

This was the birth of *What in the World are they Spraying*, which was a huge success in terms of bringing this issue out to the public. But we spoke to scientists and other people who have been collecting rainwater samples and finding that our PH had been turning from acidic in Northern California and other areas to alkaline.

This is what aluminum will do, which is the primary ingredient in geoengineering programs, and we've seen rain tests, and it'd go up as high as 50,000 percentage points in a very short period of time. So, what we're finding in our rain matches the geoengineers' proposals exactly, and it matches a number of patterns that have been designed to spray this stuff into the sky.

What we see in the sky is exactly what geoengineers state they want to do. Really, all of the negative consequences as far as the adverse weather, droughts in certain areas, and in other areas, abiotic stress. All of these consequences that geoengineers said would happen if they start these programs are now happening. We have thousands of dots that connect, and unfortunately, it is happening.

That's the very quick story. It would probably take an hour to go over my personal story of how I got involved in this. But it was really a concern. This is our planet being poisoned. And everything, every thing, and every person is breathing these aerosols in, and these heavy metals. It's now showing up in blood tests of people who have been taking them. It's very destructive to plant life and the ecosystem. So, we're seeing a collapse of all right now that's unfortunately related to geoengineering.

Q. What exactly are the effects on us humans? How would someone know if they have been infected with chem spray? Are there symptoms?

A. Well, heavy metal toxicity is especially aluminum. Alzheimer's, forgetfulness, and a number of neurological disorders, people who have been experiencing these have been going in to get blood tests and are finding that those levels have just skyrocketed.

We now have a new test that's not actually an invasive test, and we have it on my new website, *UnconventionalGrey.com*. This is a test where you can just simply swipe. It's non-invasive, and you're done. Send it in to get a full test, for a fraction of the price of a blood test, of aluminum toxicity and other heavy metals related to the geoengineering program. Then, visit with your healthcare

provider to see how to get detoxed from
this.

We see a number of illnesses, including
respiratory mortality, a number of
aluminum-related illnesses, ADD, ADHD,
all kinds of things again that are related to
the metals in the geoengineering program.
So, it's really important that we learn what
our levels are and then devise a plan to
detox.

Q. So a person can get better?

A. Absolutely. It's hard to release heavy
metals once you've been contaminated with
them. However, and you can use chlorella
or other heavy metal detox programs to get
this out and start feeling healthy because,
with every breath, we're breathing in these
aerosols. These toxins, nothing is immune
to it.

Chlorella is a food source because it is high in
protein and other essential nutrients. When
dried, it is about 45% protein, 20% fat, 20%

carbohydrate, 5% fiber, and 10% minerals and vitamins. Mass-production methods are now being used to cultivate it in large man-made circular ponds. Chlorella is consumed as a health supplement primarily in the United States and Canada and as a food supplement in Japan. Manufacturers of Chlorella products assert that it has a number of purported health effects, including an ability to treat cancer. According to the American Cancer Society, "available scientific studies do not support its effectiveness for preventing or treating cancer or any other disease in humans." A 2002 study showed that Chlorella cell walls contain lipopolysaccharides, endotoxins found in Gram-negative bacteria that affect the immune system and may cause inflammation.[1]

Q. What is the biggest effect that's happening in the world from these sprays?

A. PH changes – Aluminum Oxide will drive a soil's alkaline. So, for example, in Northern California, Dr. Francis Mangels noticed that the PH was changing in that region. And not twice as high as it should be. It was going as high as ten times the normal alkalinity. So, what happens is plant life that requires acidic soil starts to die when that PH changes. That's exactly what is happening. As a result, we have an ecosystem collapse, forest collapse, and organic foods are really having a challenge growing in this new environment.

Francis Mangels is described as "a former USDA scientist and featured expert in the movie *What in the World are they Spraying?* He is the sole person with an advanced degree in the movie. He lists his education as Ph.D. Forestry, Masters Zoology (Aquatic Insects) The University of Montana, and 35 years Federal Scientist, USDA Soil Conservation Service US Forest Service. Minors in Botany, Chemistry, Wildlife Management, and Ichthyology – http://www.youtube.com/watch?v=6vwY3wKd6Z4"

There's also an issue called "Abiotic Stress" that geoengineering creates. Abiotic Stress is really just anything that stresses the soil, whether it's PH changes or heavy metal contaminants. We didn't speak yet about how geoengineering changes our weather patterns and creates droughts and floods, but that's also an Abiotic Stress.

Abiotic stress is the negative impact of non-living factors on the living organisms in a specific environment. The non-living variable must influence the environment beyond its normal range of variation to adversely affect the population performance or individual physiology of the organism in a significant way.[2]

In the soil, what was unique, and we covered it in the film, *Why in the World are they Spraying,* was this new genetically-modified terminator seed developed by Monsanto, which grows in this new environment.

So, for example, on many organic farms, we've seen up to 60 percent of the crop loss in the past 10 to 15 years – just a huge loss of crops. So, what this does is through the death and destruction of normal and natural systems, Monsanto comes in, and they design a seed that can grow in this new environment. It's literally a hostile takeover of nature and the natural systems of God's creation.

The Monsanto Company was an American agrochemical and agricultural biotechnology corporation founded in 1901. In 2018, it was acquired by Bayer as part of its crop science division. It was headquartered in Creve Coeur, Missouri. Monsanto was most commonly known for producing genetically modified (GMO) seeds and the herbicide glyphosate known as "Roundup." They produce cotton, soy, corn, alfalfa, sorghum, and canola, which are all sprayed with Roundup to manage the surrounding weeds that may otherwise reduce how much of each crop they could.[3]

Monsanto's roles in agricultural changes, biotechnology products, lobbying of government agencies, and roots as a chemical company resulted in controversies. The company once manufactured controversial products such as the insecticide DDT, PCBs, Agent Orange, and recombinant bovine growth hormone.[4]

Bill Gates owns 500,000 shares worth 23 million US dollars (or more) of Monsanto stock.

Monsanto GMOs are banned in Germany, France, Italy, Austria, Greece, Poland, Scotland, Northern Ireland, and Belgium, among others. Also banning GMOs are Algeria and Madagascar in Africa; Turkey, Kyrgyzstan, Bhutan, and Saudi Arabia in Asia; and Belize, Peru, Ecuador, and Venezuela in the Americas.

Q. When do you think this whole geoengineering plan started?

A. 70 years ago.

Q. That long ago?

A. Yes. Technology has gotten much stronger. But it was a basic cloud seeding, weather modification, and forms of geoengineering. Full-scale deployment, though, where we started seeing the trails and started seeing 20 percent less Sun and ecosystem collapses. It looks like probably the mid-to-late 1990s when we began to see full-scale deployment.

Since that time, those of us who have been watching this closely have noticed a great increase in these programs, a great increase in aluminum-related illnesses, a great increase in terms of tree decline as the ecosystem collapses.

It's a very effective way to consolidate both monetary and political power into the hands of a few. So, these programs benefit a few at the cost of many. That's what we discussed in detail in the film, *What in the World are they Spraying?*

Cloud seeding is a type of weather modification that aims to change the amount or type of precipitation that falls from clouds by dispersing substances into the air that serve as cloud condensation or ice nuclei, which alter the microphysical processes within the cloud.

The most common chemicals used for cloud seeding include silver iodide, potassium iodide, and dry ice solid carbon dioxide. Liquid propane, which expands into a gas, has also been used. This can produce ice crystals at higher temperatures than silver iodide. After promising research, the use of hygroscopic materials, such as table salt, is becoming more popular.

Whether cloud seeding is effective in producing a statistically significant increase in precipitation is still a matter of academic debate, with contrasting results depending on the study in question and contrasting opinions among experts.

With an NFPA 704 health hazard rating of 2, silver iodide can cause temporary incapacitation or possible residual injury to humans and other mammals with intense or chronic exposure. However, there have been several detailed ecological studies that showed negligible environmental and health impacts. The toxicity of silver and silver compounds from silver iodide was shown to be of low order in some studies. These findings likely result from the minute amounts of silver generated by cloud seeding, which is about one percent of industry emissions into the atmosphere in many parts of the world, or individual exposure from tooth fillings.

In the United States, cloud seeding is used to increase precipitation in areas experiencing drought, to reduce the size of hailstones that form in thunderstorms, and to reduce the amount of fog in and around airports. In the summer of 1948, the usually humid city of Alexandria, Louisiana, under Mayor Carl B. Close, seeded a cloud with dry ice at the municipal airport during a drought, and quickly 0.85 inches of rainfall occurred.

Cloud seeding is occasionally used by major ski resorts to induce snowfall. Eleven western states and one Canadian province Alberta have ongoing weather modification operational programs. In January 2006, an $8.8 million cloud seeding project began in Wyoming to examine the effects of cloud seeding on snowfall over Wyoming's Medicine Bow, Sierra Madre, and Wind River mountain ranges.[5]

The US signed the Environmental Modification Convention in 1978, which banned the use of weather modification for hostile purposes.[6]

Many people look at the weather, and they know it's changing. We're told that it's because of C02. Well, the geoengineering factor is being left out of this equation, and it's responsible for most, if not all, of our changes in the climate.

There are many reasons for this, including selling the climate change agenda and consolidating all this money and power. We had forms of legislation, now they've built a framework to legalize geoengineering and also to erase national boundaries, state laws, and allowing an unelected body, the IPCC and the United Nations, to lead and literally micromanage our lives. A lot of this is related to geoengineering.

Q. If they started doing this about 70 years ago, did they have the same intentions back then as they do today?

A. Definitely, yes – weather control. But I also want to be respectful of other researchers looking into the many different applications of putting aerosols into the skies. So, weather control is certainly one of them and is probably one of the biggest agendas.

By putting aerosols into the sky, a lot can be achieved, whether it's military, the use of barium, one of the main components in an MRI. You get injected with barium so that the X-ray or the MRI machine can get a 3D view of your needs. These applications have military benefits. On a satellite, if you want to look into somebody's home or a compound, and there's barium literally everywhere we are, you can see and get a 3D image of what's inside of that room.

If you control the weather, which is being done, you can control the planet. Every food supply, every political system, and that is absolutely going on. Plus, selling the entire climate change agenda, which I don't think a lot of people are aware of the personal implications this has. Also, the national implications. These programs are erasing national boundaries.

We've had some historic legislation, which nobody's talking about. Except for us, and geoengineering relates directly to this. Because again, geoengineering is changing our climate and all of the climate models that we are basing all of these taxes. All of these changes, including monitoring us in the home, are based on climate models that are projecting and noticing that our climate has been changing.

Geoengineering programs are designed to change the temperature of the planet. They're designed to manipulate our weather. They are not included in geoengineering models. But these models are being used to initiate all of these changes, including a multi-trillion-dollar transfer of wealth. This wealth has to come from somewhere. It comes from you through taxes, through mandates, and again in the United States and many other countries around the world, we have elected officials, and they have the ability to represent their constituents.

The climate change, the COP 21, which passed in December of 2015, created the framework to remove our representative's ability to legislate us. What it did was create the framework to legalize geoengineering into tax mandate, and it really created an unelected body that will micromanage our lives.

The Paris Agreement is a legally binding international treaty on climate change. It was adopted by 196 Parties at COP 21 in Paris on December 12, 2015, and entered into force on November 4, 2016. Its goal is to limit global warming to well below 2, preferably to 1.5 degrees Celsius, compared to pre-industrial levels.[7]

On December 12, 2015, the participating 196 countries agreed, by consensus, to the final global pact, the Paris Agreement, to reduce emissions as part of the method for reducing greenhouse gas. In the 12-page document, the members agreed to reduce their carbon output as soon as possible and to do their best to keep global warming to well below 2 °C.[8]

In the course of the debates, island states of the Pacific, Seychelles, but also the Philippines, their very existence threatened by sea-level rise, had strongly voted for setting a goal of 1.5 °C instead of only 2 °C.

France's Foreign Minister, Laurent Fabius, said this "ambitious and balanced" plan was a "historic turning point" in the goal of reducing global warming. However, some others criticized the fact that significant sections are promises or aims and not firm commitments by the countries.[9]

Q. Is there any way we can change this? Is there no going back?

A. The reason for me releasing *Unconventional Grey* is because we're in a state of emergency. I'd say a legal and legislative state of emergency. It's critical that we address this immediately. Our strategy is this: we have the framework to initiate what we call the "Aerosol Collection Project." We are planning on doing the first test, where we go up into the trails, test the aerosols, and then bring these findings, which we're confident we'll prove conclusively that geoengineering is occurring and it is changing our climate.

Our objectives are to, with the help of Dr. Marvin Herndon, who will be writing the peer-reviewed paper of our project. Our goals are to create a legal model to be used in courtrooms around the world to get court injunctions, to stop any climate change laws, climate change mandates, and climate change legislation. This includes geoengineering until we do not test positive for geoengineering.

James Marvin Herndon, born in 1944, is an American interdisciplinary scientist who earned his BA degree in physics in 1970 from the University of California, San Diego, and his Ph.D. degree in nuclear chemistry in 1974 from Texas A&M University. For three years, J. Marvin Herndon was a post-doctoral assistant to Hans Suess and Harold C. Urey in geochemistry and cosmo-chemistry at the University of California, San Diego.

Herndon has become a proponent of the chemtrail conspiracy theory and published several peer-reviewed papers claiming that coal fly ash is being sprayed for geoengineering.

In 2016, two of his papers, however, were retracted because of flaws. Herndon disputed the reason for retraction, claiming the retractions were "a well-organized effort of the CIA to deceive. Those concerted efforts to cause said retractions prove that the high officials who ordered the spraying know very well that they are poisoning humanity and want to hide that fact."[10]

So, that we can prove that the climate models are wrong, and based on that model, we can demand that the geoengineering is stopped. It's an interesting strategy because while the goals are to stop geoengineering, it has the ability, and these are the objectives, to stop the whole New World Order global governance agenda, which is all predicated on these bogus climate models.

The common theme in conspiracy theories about a "New World Order" is that a secretive power elite with a globalist agenda is conspiring to eventually rule the world through an authoritarian world government, which will replace sovereign nation-states and all-encompassing propaganda whose ideology hails the establishment of the New World Order as the culmination of history's progress.

Many influential historical and contemporary figures have therefore been alleged to be part of a cabal that operates through many front organizations to orchestrate significant political and financial events, ranging from causing systemic crises to pushing through controversial policies, at both national and international levels, as steps in an ongoing plot to achieve world domination.

Before the early 1990s, New World Order conspiracist was limited to two American countercultures, primarily the militantly anti-government right and secondarily that part of fundamentalist Christianity concerned with the end-time emergence of the Antichrist.

American televangelist Pat Robertson, with his 1991 bestselling book *The New World Order*, became the most prominent Christian disseminator of conspiracy theories about recent American history. He described a scenario where Wall Street, the Federal Reserve System, the Council on Foreign Relations, the Bilderberg Group, and the Trilateral Commission controlled the flow of events from behind the scenes, nudging people constantly and covertly in the direction of world government for the Antichrist.

From the mid-1990s to the early 2000s, Hollywood conspiracy-thriller television shows and films also played a role in introducing a general audience to various fringe and esoteric theories related to New World Order conspiracist, which by that point had developed to include black helicopters, FEMA "concentration camps," etc. theories which for decades previously were confined to largely right-wing subcultures.

Conspiracy theorists believe that the New World Order will also be implemented through the use of human population control in order to monitor and control the movement of individuals more easily. The means range from stopping the growth of human societies through reproductive health and family planning programs, which promote abstinence, contraception, and abortion, or intentionally reducing the bulk of the world population through genocides by mongering unnecessary wars, through plagues by engineering emergent viruses and tainting vaccines, and through environmental disasters by controlling the weather, HAARP, chemtrails, etc.

Conspiracy theorists argue that globalists plotting on behalf of a New World Order are neo-Malthusians, who engage in overpopulation and climate change alarmism in order to create public support for coercive population control and ultimately world government. Agenda 21 is condemned as "re-concentrating" people into urban areas and depopulating rural ones, even generating a dystopian novel by Glenn Beck where single-family homes are a distant memory.[11]

What it also does is there are certain regions that certain corporations are completely losing power due to climate change legislation and climate change agenda. Even those that are supportive of this will now have a vested interest in demanding that geoengineering is stopped.

I'm quite certain that when we see geoengineering stopped, we will see our planet come back into balance, and we will find that there is not a global warming issue. But I really want to make a strong statement, I won't argue whether the planet is warming or cooling, and the reason is this, you can't determine if the planet is warming or cooling until geoengineering is stopped. That is not arguable.

Q. Who is behind this specifically?

A. Many different governments and many different corporations. So, right now, we have the IPCC of the United Nations, who is pushing for the legalization of geoengineering, and of course, they are sponsored by a number of corporations and also a number of governments.

The IPCC is the Intergovernmental Panel on Climate Change, an intergovernmental body of the United Nations that is dedicated to providing the world with objective, scientific information relevant to understanding.[12]

However, we will soon find out who is geoengineering if we allow this climate change agenda to mature. If we do that, then they will mandate it due to a state of emergency. The Obama administration has stated that climate change is a national security threat.

They're now even talking about suing the FBI, who are quote, "Climate change deniers." They're trying to remove our ability to address this issue because it's the key to this transfer of wealth, to this transfer of power, and enslaving the world.

This is America. How can you take away our freedom of speech? Because America has been done away with. The Obama administration has announced the U.N. troops were coming onto American soil.

What does that mean? Now they're talking about removing our freedom of speech. They are not coming to protect our constitutional rights. They are coming to enforce the United Nations' agenda because people with freedom are not going to be supportive of this. They are coming with handcuffs, and they are coming with guns. Our time is very short to address this, and if this rings true to anybody, we need support for these initiatives and to complete *Unconventional Grey*.

Q. What do you think the time frame is? How much time do we have?

A. Five year planned implementation. Now Attorney General Lynch is looking into prosecuting climate change deniers. Our time is now, and that's probably the best way to put this.

Q. Can you describe the mechanics of this? How did they get the chemicals in the air?

A. Many different ways. Sometimes we get stuck in this idea that it's either this or that. I've seen this argument come in. Well, it's in the jet fuel. No, it's the Welsbach Patent. There are many ways that they are doing this.

Welsbach seeding is a patented climate engineering method involving seeding the stratosphere with small 10-to-100-micron metal oxide particles, thorium dioxide, Aluminum oxide. The purpose of the Welsbach seeding would be to reduce atmospheric warming due to the greenhouse effect resulting from a greenhouse gases layer by converting radiative energy at near-infrared wavelengths into radiation at far-infrared wavelengths, permitting some of the converted radiation to escape into space, thus cooling the atmosphere. The seeding as described would be performed by airplanes at altitudes between 7 and 13 kilometers.[13]

There are many different ways, including spraying from airplanes. I just mentioned the Welsbach Patent. That was a device designed specifically to spray metals for geoengineering purposes, not our sky. There's evidence now that they are putting in some aluminum and other related materials in the jet fuel – platform-based aerosol distributions in the form of cloud generations.

What we do know is that in order to achieve the weather modifications, the weather control objectives requires certain elements of aluminum, barium, perhaps coal fly ash, and a number of other things that are very effective in this.

Coal Fly Ash is the finely divided residue that results from the combustion of pulverized coal and is transported from the combustion chamber by exhaust gases. Over 61 million metric tons (68 million tons) of fly ash were produced in 2001. Where does fly ash come from? Fly ash is produced by coal-fired electric and steam generating plants. Typically, coal is pulverized and blown with air into the boiler's combustion chamber, where it immediately ignites, generating heat and producing a molten mineral residue.

Boiler tubes extract heat from the boiler, cooling the flue gas and causing the molten mineral residue to harden and form ash.

Where is fly ash used? Currently, over 20 million metric tons of fly ash are used annually in a variety of engineering applications. Typical highway engineering applications include Portland cement concrete (PCC), soil and road base stabilization, flowable fills, grouts, structural fill, and asphalt filler.

Fly ash utilization, especially in concrete, has significant environmental benefits, including increasing the life of concrete roads and structures by improving concrete durability, the net reduction in energy use and greenhouse gas and other adverse air emissions when fly ash is used to replace or displace manufactured cement, reduction in the amount of coal combustion products that must be disposed of in landfills, and conservation of other natural resources and materials.[14]

Q. What exactly is found in the chemtrails?

A. Aluminum, Barium, Sulfur, Dioxide. These are the ones we put out there. A lot of people around the world started testing the rain. Those who did full panels were finding arsenic, and they are finding manganese. I met with Dr. Marvin Herndon, a world-renowned physicist, and Dr. Herndon found evidence that they are utilizing coal fly ash. This is a toxic substance that is trapped after coal is burnt. The FDA has very stringent ways to trap this, and I think it's similar to the fluoride issue, which is very toxic. It's very effective for geoengineering, and now it looks like it's implemented in geoengineering programs.

Fluoride toxicity is a condition in which there are elevated levels of the fluoride ion in the body. Although fluoride is safe for dental health at low concentrations, sustained consumption of large amounts of soluble fluoride salts is dangerous. Referring to a common salt of fluoride, sodium fluoride (NaF), the lethal dose for most adult humans is estimated at 5 to 10 g, which is equivalent to 32 to 64 mg elemental fluoride/kg body weight.

Ingestion of fluoride can produce gastrointestinal discomfort at doses at least 15 to 20 times lower 0.2–0.3 mg/kg or 10 to 15 mg for a 50 kg person than lethal doses. Although it is helpful topically for dental health in low dosage, chronic ingestion of fluoride in large amounts interferes with bone formation. In this way, the most widespread examples of fluoride poisoning arise from the consumption of groundwater that is abnormally fluoride rich.[15]

Q. You believe that these chemtrails are what's causing the drought in California?

A. Yes, definitely. We've had this polar vortex, so by putting aerosols into our atmosphere, what the establishment can do is through the use of HARRP-related or HARRP technologies, they can heat up these heavy metals because they're conductors.

What this does is if we heat up part of the atmosphere, it will expand, essentially create a bubble. So, the weather that normally comes into California when it hits this bubble will divert north. What it does is bring all of the moisture that normally comes into California and brings it up into the Arctic, and including bringing up warm air into that region.

Any stream, whether it's the jet stream or river, seeks to correct itself. So, after the warm air goes up into the Arctic, it comes back down into the Midwest. I was in Chicago for about a year and a half, and it was very rainy, very cold, and a lot of precipitation. The jet stream was rebounding back, bringing all of these weather systems in. So, as a result, very warm temperatures in California, very warm in the Arctic, but then downstream very cold.

HARRP (The High-frequency Active Auroral Research Program) was initiated as an ionospheric research program jointly funded by the U.S. Air Force, the U.S. Navy, the University of Alaska Fairbanks, and the Defense Advanced

Research Projects Agency. It was designed and built by BAE Advanced Technologies.

HAARP is the subject of numerous conspiracy theories. Various individuals have speculated about the hidden motivations and capabilities of the project. For example, Rosalie Bertell warned in 1996 about the deployment of HAARP as a military weapon. Michel Chossudovsky stated in a book published by the Committee on Monetary and Economic Reform that "recent scientific evidence suggests that HAARP is fully operational and has the capability of triggering floods, hurricanes, droughts, and earthquakes."

Over time, HAARP has been blamed for generating such catastrophes, as well as thunderstorms, in Iran, Pakistan, Haiti, Turkey, Greece, and the Philippines, and even major power outages, the downing of TWA Flight 800, Gulf War syndrome, and chronic fatigue syndrome.[16]

Stanford University professor Umran Inan told *Popular Science* that weather-control conspiracy theories were "completely uninformed," explaining that "there's absolutely nothing we can do to disturb the Earth's weather systems.

Even though the power HAARP radiates is very large, it's minuscule compared with the power of a lightning flash—and there are 50 to 100 lightning flashes every second. HAARP's intensity is very small." Computer scientist David Naiditch characterizes HAARP as "a magnet for conspiracy theorists," saying that HAARP attracts their attention because "its purpose seems deeply mysterious to the scientifically uninformed."[17]

Then, we look into the Agenda 2030 issue, and this is directly related because what Governor Jerry Brown did was due to this drought, they put mandates on certain people. They've called for a state of emergency, which gives Jerry Brown, through eminent domain, the legal right to take anybody's property.

They also have been privatizing waters, so if there's a lack of water, which Agenda 2030 has objectives of literally controlling every natural resource on the planet. So, Jerry Brown, instead of allowing the water to flow to the smaller farms, where smaller family farms have had rights to water for generations, now he has taken that away from them and given water to the big corporate ad companies.

So, the smaller farmers dry up, go out of business, and are forced to sell their farms for pennies on the dollar. So, there's no question about it, this is very beneficial to the big corporations, and they are making water their next oil.

I think we're going to continue to see this go into other States and see the same corporate game plan. They have the ability to do this, and this is what's happening.

One major objective of the Agenda 21 initiative is that every local government should draw its own local Agenda 21. Its aim initially was to achieve global sustainable development by 2000, with the "21" in Agenda 21 referring to the original target of the 21st century. The Agenda is a commitment to eradicate poverty and achieve sustainable development by 2030 worldwide, ensuring that no one is left behind.

The adoption of the 2030 Agenda was a landmark achievement, providing for a shared global vision towards sustainable development for all.[18]

The 17 sustainable development goals to transform our world:

- GOAL 1: No Poverty
- GOAL 2: Zero Hunger
- GOAL 3: Good Health and Well-being
- GOAL 4: Quality Education
- GOAL 5: Gender Equality
- GOAL 6: Clean Water and Sanitation
- GOAL 7: Affordable and Clean Energy
- GOAL 8: Decent Work and Economic Growth
- GOAL 9: Industry, Innovation, and Infrastructure
- GOAL 10: Reduced Inequality
- GOAL 11: Sustainable Cities and Communities
- GOAL 12: Responsible Consumption and Production
- GOAL 13: Climate Action
- GOAL 14: Life Below Water
- GOAL 15: Life on Land

- GOAL 16: Peace and Justice Strong Institutions
- GOAL 17: Partnerships to achieve the Goal

But the fears Agenda 21 has provoked plug directly into more than a century of far-right worries about any international body imposing any kind of control on the United States.

Q. You say that this is going on around the world, and other countries are involved also?

A. Absolutely. We see trails over most regions, but not all, though. There are a couple of areas in Africa. But I want to be very clear: controlling the weather here in the United States can have very profound effects in Europe. There is nothing that is not touched by these programs.

Q. What should people be doing right now?

A. Supporting our efforts. We need to get planes up in the sky. Again, we have rain tests from all around the world, but that's not going to fly in court. We need aerosol samples. It's imperative that we get this into court immediately. We have a legal team ready. We just need financial support to do filings and move forward with this.

Q. So, you actually want to send planes up and follow those planes that are spraying and get samples from them?

A. Absolutely. What's interesting is we have rain tests from around the world, and those rain tests have the exact fingerprint of geoengineering programs in them. We're extremely confident, however, in a court of law, and conclusively proving is a different ball game. Nobody has ever gone up in a trail and tested for geoengineering material. So, that is our objective.

Q. What about the scientific community? How do they feel about this?

A. Largely, they've denied that it's going on because they're driven by grant money. The official statement by many, not all, though, we have many Ph.D.s, many credentialed former EPA, just a number of credentialed people who are on-board.

However, many of the universities, the establishment scientists, are not funded. They have not looked into this. So, if you take the EPA as an example, the EPA official statement is, "We have found no evidence to indicate that geoengineering is happening."

You know what? I have to admit that the EPA is right. They haven't found any evidence to indicate that geoengineering is happening. You know why? Because they haven't looked for it. I have found no evidence that anybody is driving a car in Los Angeles right now. However, I haven't looked outside today and witnessed anybody because I haven't looked. Now, if I looked, I think there's a pretty good chance that I will see somebody driving. But if I don't, I won't find any evidence. That's where we're at. They haven't looked for it. They haven't tested for it. As a matter of fact, they quit testing for combustibles a number of years ago. They quit testing for the primary ingredients in geoengineering programs, I believe, ten years ago.

We have this issue of cap and trade, which is a scheme to cap every American to get them tightly packed into cities through Agenda 21 objectives. We will all have to cut down the amount of carbon that we use. Most of us live today, where we are somewhat conservative in what we use. I turn my lights off and everything.

But through the Smart Meters, they now have the ability to determine what appliances you are using, when you're using, how much you're using, and what they will be doing is levying fines. They will say that you are only allowed to use, let's say today you are using 100 units of carbon, we're now going to cap you at 40. Any number you go over, you're going to get a bill.

So, for example, let's say if you leave a light on and you go on vacation. The Smart Meter recognizes that you left a light on, and you can get fined $400. Let's say you use a vacuum in your home, the one that you bought last year. It's a great vacuum. The Smart Meter says that it wasn't a United Nations-mandated vacuum. It's not clean. We're going to fine you $200, plus if you use it again, we're going to fine you $400.

Now, you have to buy the new one, whether it's General Electric or whatever company that makes a green vacuum cleaner. That's the one that you have to use. This is the United Nations through corporations, which is a dream for corporations to control what you do, when you do it, and what you use in your home.

In Oregon, they now have a mileage tax. Again, you're going to be capped. So, let's say that you live 15 miles away from work. You're going to have to cut down on how much you drive. You might be able to drive to and from work. But driving anywhere else, sorry, you've got to take public transportation. I'm sorry, you went over your mileage. You're going to be charged $10 for every additional mile that you use.

That's how they are going to cap people's carbon usage. This is a dictatorial plan. It is an Orwellian plan, and it will impact each and every part of our lives. By the way, it is a whole new monetary economic system that is carbon-based. We will all be pushed into poverty because of this.

This is anti-life. This is anti-freedom. And the key to this whole thing is geoengineering. Because geoengineering, not CO_2, is creating most of the changes in our climate, and it's not included in climate change models.

All of this is a huge transfer of wealth, loss of rights, loss of property because property has a carbon value. You're going to be taxed through the roof if you have five acres. Now, you can only have an eighth of an acre, and you're still going to be taxed through the roof. It is an agenda to also steal people's land.

Q. What you're saying is that the people who are out protesting about climate change are doing the wrong thing then?

A. Absolutely. I have a very simple way to end climate change. That's stopping geoengineering. When somebody is out there saying, "Save our Planet," it is really paying somebody. It is really allowing somebody to fine us for our actions in our own homes. Our privacy is gone. Do people realize? They don't.

If we have a specific list of what is being planned, and I was in Paris over the summer and handed it out to all of these activists who are demanding that our legators do more, I guarantee you that they would not be supportive of any of the legislative steps to bring this in.

They are selling their children and the world into enslavement without even knowing.

Listen to the full interview with Michael Murphy on my website:

www.alanrwarren.com/hom-
podcast-
episodes/episode/b43ac247/what-
in-the-world-are-they-spraying-
michaek-murphy

Interview Afterthoughts

So that long-lasting condensation trails are "chemtrails" consisting of chemical or biological agents left in the sky by high-flying aircraft, sprayed for nefarious purposes, and undisclosed to the general public. But the science behind those trails left by jet planes isn't that difficult to understand.

Contrails, or condensation trails, are "streaks of condensed water vapor created in the air by an airplane or rocket at high altitudes." Fossil fuel combustion, as in piston and jet engines, produces carbon dioxide and water vapor.

At high altitudes, the air is very cold. Hot, humid air from the engine exhaust mixes with the colder surrounding air, causing the water vapor to condense into droplets or ice crystals that form visible clouds. The rate at which contrails dissipate is entirely dependent on weather conditions.[19]

The conspiracy theorists never can tell us how they get pilots involved in this or even why they would be. As well, the issue of faked evidence has arisen, whereby pictures and videos presented online from pilots releasing chemical trails from their planes into the sky above us. These were later found to have been falsified.[20] When you actually have to create fake evidence, you can no longer trust those that created it. They are no longer trustworthy.

A lot of the so-called "scientific tests" made on land that had been sprayed by these chemtrails showed high levels of barium and other chemicals. Anybody who has ever done tests on these grounds has found the same numbers since so many of these chemicals are naturally occurring on the Earth.

As of late, the conspiracy theorists behind chemtrails have decided that using that term has been successfully debunked. So, they are now using the term "anti-geoengineering." In their minds, the deep state, under the guidance of Bill Gates and Monsanto, is causing global warming because of their geoengineering.

Bottom line: The Chemtrails Conspiracy Theory maps pretty closely to the origin and growth of the internet, where you can still find a number of websites that promote this particular brand of pseudoscience.[21]

---

1. Chlorella - Wikipedia. https://en.wikipedia.org/wiki/Chlorella
2. Abiotic stress - Wikipedia. https://en.wikipedia.org/wiki/Abiotic_stress
3. MONSATAN: a Monsanto Documentary - GoyimTV. https://www.goyimtv.tv/v/1034568045/MONSATAN--a-Monsanto-Documentary
4. Monsanto - Wikipedia. https://en.wikipedia.org/wiki/Monsanto_public_relations_activities
5. A Medley of Potpourri: Cloud seeding. https://amedleyofpotpourri.blogspot.com/2020/11/cloud-seeding.html
6. Cloud seeding - Wikipedia. https://en.wikipedia.org/wiki/Cloud_seeding
7. UTSA climatologist to fight greenhouse gases in San https://www.utsa.edu/today/2021/01/story/debbage-caap-2021.html
8. PA 's Climate Plan – frackorporation. https://frackorporation.wordpress.com/2015/12/16/pa-s-climate-plan/

9. 2015 United Nations Climate Change Conference - Wikipedia. https://en.wikipedia.org/wiki/2015_United_Nations_Climate_Change_Conference

10. J. Marvin Herndon - Wikipedia. https://en.wikipedia.org/wiki/J._Marvin_Herndon

11. New World Order (conspiracy theory) - Wikipedia. https://en.wikipedia.org/wiki/New_World_Order_conspiracy_theories

12. RESOLUTION - Granicus. https://honolulu.granicus.com/MetaViewer.php?view_id=&event_id=461&meta_id=85271

13. Chemtrails – Geoengineering | nextexx. https://nextexx.com/2020/02/15/chemtrails-geoengineering/

14. Chapter 1 - Fly Ash - An Engineering Material - Fly Ash https://www.fhwa.dot.gov/pavement%20/recycling/fach01.cfm

15. Fluoride toxicity - Wikipedia. https://en.wikipedia.org/wiki/Fluoride_toxicity

16. High-frequency Active Auroral Research Program - Wikipedia. https://en.wikipedia.org/wiki/HAARP

17. Holes In Heaven? HAARP and Advances in Tesla Technology .... https://documentaryheaven.com/holes-in-heaven-haarp-and-advances-in-tesla-technology/

18. The 2030 Agenda for Sustainable Development and SDGs .... https://ec.europa.eu/environment/sustainable-development/SDGs/index_en.htm

19. Chemtrail conspiracy theory - Wikipedia. https://en.wikipedia.org/wiki/Chemtrail_theory

20. UK Poisoning: Russia Recycles Responses | by @DFRLab https://medium.com/dfrlab/uk-poisoning-russia-recycles-responses-77e1d357b777

21. Scientists Published An Article On 'Chemtrails' (They Aren https://www.forbes.com/sites/daviddisalvo/2016/08/14/are-conspiracy-theorists-right-about-nefarious-chemtrails/

Hitler Escaped the Bunker

The Conspiracy Theory

Probably, the first major conspiracy theory that came out in the 20th century was that surrounding the death of Adolph Hitler. Understandably, after the war ended, people were left in a state of shock. This was the war that touched everybody by killing and unsettling the foundation of society. Hitler had risen to power and had influence over so many people, just like a God.

Could a man like that really be dead?

The fear had worked its way through all parts of society, including the President of the United States and the FBI. The American government had so little trust in the Soviet Union, and without having Hitler's body, inside everybody's mind was the possibility that Hitler not only survived but relocated to Argentina and was starting his fourth Reich.

In the last ten years, this theory became so mainstream that there were several new books written. Even a two-part mini-series, *Hunting Hitler*, produced by the Arts & Entertainment Network. So, why now was it gaining so much attention in the mainstream of society?

Interview with Gerrard Williams

In order to get a good answer to that question, I approached the author and filmmaker Gerrard Williams who had been at the forefront of this investigation since the beginning. I was able to do two interviews with Williams in 2014 and 2015. These are the highlights of both interviews.

Gerrard Williams has been an International Television Journalist and filmmaker for over 30 years. He has covered most of the top international news stories of the last 20 years, including the fall of the Soviet Union, the war in Yugoslavia, the Rwanda Genocide, the first Gulf War, the aftermath of the second, and the U.S. occupation of Iraq, and the 2004 Tsunami.

He has recently made documentary films in Kenya, Argentina, and Albania, which have been broadcast by Al-Jazeera International, SIC in Portugal, Channel 4 News in the U.K., and SKY News. He is currently post-producing a major Drama-Documentary, *Grey Wolf*, and is developing various feature film proposals.

Grey Wolf: The Escape of Adolph Hitler – The book and film concern the allegations by its makers that Adolf Hitler did not die in his Berlin bunker in 1945, but escaped, along with Eva Braun and several other Nazi officials, to Argentina and lived ten kilometers east of Bariloche. According to the filmmakers, Hitler's escape was organized by Martin Bormann, who also fled to Argentina and was aided and abetted by the Government of Juan Perón. The film also alleges that American intelligence agencies were aware Hitler was in Argentina, and that significant funds were taken from Germany to Argentina, and that these were later stolen by Bormann. The film alleges that Hitler died in Argentina alone, poor, and mentally ill in 1962, leaving behind a wife and at least one child.[1]

Hunting Hitler is a History Channel television series – According to documents that were declassified by the FBI in 2014, Adolf Hitler may have survived World War II and fled to South America following the fall of Nazi Germany. In this series, a team of investigators, led by 21-year CIA veteran Bob Baer and war crimes investigator John Cencich, undertakes a definitive search with the goal of finding out whether the notorious dictator actually survived the war and pulled off one of history's greatest disappearing acts. The team uncovers a mysterious Nazi lair in the Argentinean jungle and searches for evidence of a missing U-boat that may have transported Hitler out of Europe as Germany collapsed. The first episode date was November 10, 2015, and the final episode date was February 20, 2018.[2]

Q. How long does it take to do the research in a project like this?

A. The research for *Grey Wolf* took Simon (Dunstan – co-author) and me about five years, 18 trips to Argentina, a couple of trips to America, trips to Berlin, and a great deal of time and money spent.

Q. How did you get into this story?

A. This all started off when I was doing other documentaries in Argentina for British broadcasters. It's my background, television news, and I came across this story that Adolf Hitler had escaped to Argentina on a submarine at the end of the war. I thought, "You know I've never done a stupid story. I've never done a silly story." I had always done serious stories. I did Iraq twice, Rwanda, all the rest of the major stories of the 20th Century. So, I thought I would do a half-hour conspiracy theory film and see if I could sell it to the History Channel or whoever.

Then, we started to look at and talk to people. And in Argentina, the majority of people, because they've been so used to growing up with former Nazis and former

fascists from Europe and their children,
nobody was surprised at all. In fact, a lot of
people said, "Yes, I know this, and
everybody here knows it." That's when we
started to take it seriously. We started to
look at it and think there was a lot more to
this than meets the eye.

We went back and started to look at the
contemporary news reporting from people
like the Associated Press, Reuters, United
Press International, and they were all
reporting very different things to the story
that's being told in the last 70 odd years.
They were saying that "Stalin said he
escaped to Spain or Argentina." General
Zhukov, at the time, said, "Yes, we can find
no body that is Adolf Hitler's." The BBC
that was in the bunker with the Soviet
troops when they took it said they could
find no bodies that could have been Adolf
Hitler. They were offered six poor doubles
of Hitler.

General Georgy Konstantinovich Zhukov was a
Soviet general and Marshal of the Soviet Union.

He also served as Chief of the General Staff, Minister of Defense, and was a member of the Presidium of the Communist Party (later Politburo). During the Second World War, Zhukov oversaw some of the Red Army's most decisive victories.[3]

So, it started to become something that I was initially completely shocked at because I hadn't been a journalist for 30 odd years. I'd covered lots and lots of stories, and I had never seen one like this, where what was reported at the time and what we've been told historically are completely and totally different.

Q. Tell us about your co-author of the book, Simon Dunstan?

A. Simon is a military historian. He's one of the world's leading experts on the armored fighting vehicle. When I first took this to him, he said, "Don't be mad. One, you will ruin your own reputation. Two, I'll never be able to write a book again." Then, he looked at the research I had, and he started to do his own research and said, "We have to do this. What we've been told is wrong."

I think the evidence is quite substantial what we had in *Grey Wolf* and what we found out since. The real story is Hitler did not die in the bunker in Berlin. He didn't commit suicide. He escaped. It was well organized, and it was well planned. He escaped to a country, which was the only other country in the world that had a Nazi party – Argentina.

He lived out his life, and not very happy, luckily. I'd hate to think that anything pleasant happened to him. But he lived out his life until 1962 in Argentina. Then, he died of natural causes. But there was no heroic suicide in the bunker in Berlin.

Q. Besides saving his own life, what was the purpose of his escape? Do you think he was going to try and carry on with the Nazi party?

A. I think it's quite confusing or difficult this one. The real brain behind this was Martin Bormann, who also didn't die in

Berlin. Bormann had been planning this since the early 1940s. In 1943, he put the whole Operation Paperclip into gear.

———————————————————————

"Operation Paperclip" was a secret program of the Joint Intelligence Objectives Agency largely carried out by special agents of Army CIC, in which more than 1,600 German scientists, engineers, and technicians, such as Wernher von Braun and his V-2 rocket team, were taken from Germany to the United States, for U.S. government employment, primarily between 1945 and 1959. Many were former members, and some were former leaders of the Nazi Party. The primary purpose for Operation Paperclip was U.S. military advantage in the Soviet-American Cold War and the "Space Race." The Soviet Union was more aggressive in forcibly recruiting more than 2,200 German specialists, a total of more than 6,000 people including family members with Operation Osoaviakhim during one night on October 22, 1946.[4]

I think at one stage, Hitler was central to what he was thinking – that there was a possibility the Reich could re-establish itself at some point in the future. Hitler was very central to that. I think that the reason for Hitler escaping, it's somewhat confusing.

Martin Bormann, who is the real key to this, he's the money man. He's the guy who actually runs the Nazi party. Bormann worshipped Hitler, so there was a very good personal reason for Bormann wanting to get Hitler out. I think, at one stage, it was thought by him that Hitler might have been the right figurehead to lead a new Nazi or a new fourth Reich from Argentina.

I think what happened, though, in real terms, was that once Hitler had escaped and Bormann realized how the world had been impacted by what the Nazis did in the camps, murdering 11 million people, never mind what they did on the Eastern Front. Bormann realized that the whole party, the whole "brand" being led by Adolf Hitler, would never work again.

It didn't really matter to Bormann anyways. He controlled the money. He managed to get billions out of Germany and a great deal more, including artwork and many other industrial things that were needed. Not physically, but they were transferred electronically. In those days, much the same way that we can do now, the Swiss banks helped them out and took their 6 percent as they always do on every transaction.

Bormann was in a position when he came out to Germany in 1947, where his political structure was intact, and he could influence the rise of a new Germany. That's exactly what happened. The Nazis funded what became known as the West German economic miracle. There's no economic miracle in West Germany after the war. The Germans don't work harder than the Americans, or the British, or the French, or anybody else. What they did have was huge amounts of capital that had been shipped out by the Nazis and then were brought back in to fund the rebuilding of the German industry. That's why Germany today is Europe's biggest economic powerhouse.

So, Hitler became pretty much a sideline from 1946 on. He wasn't very well, and Bormann was the man with his hands on the purse strings, with his hands on the information and the contacts. They used to call him the "Information General" or the "Telex General" is a better way to put that. He was in contact with everybody, and he never wore a uniform. He never took rank in the army.

Martin Ludwig Bormann was a German Nazi Party official and head of the Nazi Party Chancellery. He gained immense power by using his position as Adolf Hitler's private secretary to control the flow of information and access to Hitler. After Hitler's suicide on April 30, 1945, he was Party Minister of the National Socialist German Workers' Party.

At around 11:00 pm on May 1st, Bormann left the Führerbunker with SS doctor Ludwig Stumpfegger, Hitler Youth leader Artur Axmann, and Hitler's pilot Hans Baur as members of one of the groups attempting to break out of the Soviet encirclement. Bormann carried with him a copy of Hitler's last will and testament. The group left the Führerbunker and traveled on foot via a U-Bahn subway tunnel to the Friedrichstraße station, where they surfaced.

Several members of the party attempted to cross the Spree River at the Weidendammer Bridge while crouching behind a Tiger tank. The tank was hit by an anti-tank round, and Bormann and Stumpfegger were knocked to the ground. Bormann, Stumpfegger, and several others eventually crossed the river on their third attempt.

Bormann, Stumpfegger, and Axmann walked along the railway tracks to Lehrter station, where Axmann decided to leave the others and go in the opposite direction. When he encountered a Red Army patrol, Axmann doubled back. He saw two bodies, which he later identified as Bormann and Stumpfegger, on a bridge near the railway switching yard. He did not have time to check thoroughly, so he did not know how they died. Since the Soviets never admitted to finding Bormann's body, his fate remained in doubt for many years.

During the chaotic days after the war, contradictory reports arose as to Bormann's whereabouts. Sightings were reported in Argentina, Spain, and elsewhere. Bormann's wife was placed under surveillance in case he tried to contact her. Jakob Glas, Bormann's long-time chauffeur, insisted that he saw Bormann in Munich in July 1946. In case Bormann was still alive, multiple public notices about the upcoming Nuremberg trials were placed in newspapers and on the radio in October and November 1945 to notify him of the proceedings against him.

The trial got underway on November 20, 1945. Lacking evidence confirming Bormann's death, the International Military Tribunal tried him in absentia, as permitted under Article 12 of their charter. He was charged with three counts: conspiracy to wage a war of aggression, war crimes, and crimes against humanity.[5]

Over the years, several organizations, including the CIA and the West German Government, attempted to locate Bormann without success. In 1964, the West German government offered a reward of 100,000 Deutsche Marks for information leading to Bormann's capture.

In 1963, a retired postal worker named Albert Krumnow told police that around May 8, 1945, the Soviets had ordered him and his colleagues to bury two bodies found near the railway bridge near Lehrter station.

Excavations on 20–21 July 1965 at the site specified by Axmann and Krumnow failed to locate the bodies. However, on December 7, 1972, construction workers uncovered human remains near Lehrter station in West Berlin, just 39 feet from the spot where Krumnow claimed he had buried them.[6]

The remains were conclusively identified as Bormann's in 1998 when German authorities ordered genetic testing on fragments of the skull. Bormann's remains were cremated, and his ashes were scattered in the Baltic Sea on 16 August 1999.[7]

Q. Adolf Hitler went by a wolf name, didn't he? I think it was the "Noble Wolf."

A. His secret name was always "Mr. Wolf." When he was introduced to Eva Braun, he was introduced to her as "Mr. Wolf." She also used to call him "Uncle Wolf." Most of the bases around the Nazi-occupied territories all had "wolf" in the title, so it would be the "Wolf's Lair," or the "Wolf's Bane," and his plane was the "Flying Wolf." He had a bit of fixation because the name Adolf means "Noble Wolf" in German. Not that I think there was anything noble about this criminal.

Q. So, did Eva Braun go to Argentina with Hitler?

A. Yes.

Q Did she stay with Hitler until he died?

A. No. They already had a child in Germany, who would have been about six or seven at the end of the war, and who came out to join them in Argentina. Our research has shown that Eva Braun was in every early stage of pregnancy in the bunker in 1945. She then had a child in Argentina, either in December or January of 1946.

So, they had two little girls living with them. But she was a lot younger than Hitler. He was 55 or 56, and she was in her twenties when they left Berlin.

I think that hiding away in the foothills of the Andes Mountains was something that an immensely wealthy young woman, who had enjoyed parties and traveling around Europe when the Nazis were at their height, was something that she didn't want to put up with anymore. So, from our research, we understand that she left him in the fifties and took the children to live elsewhere in Argentina. She spent a lot of time in her later life, in Buenos Aires, but that was well after Hitler had died.

Q. Did you find out how Hitler died and where he was buried?

A. Again, people have said that that would be the smoking gun. If you could find Hitler's remains, you can then get DNA and get that DNA checked against other surviving relatives of Hitler or against his sister, who is buried at Berchtesgaden in Bavaria.

I think, and this is something that we haven't been able to firm up, but we've had various unconfirmed reports that his body was cremated. The last thing Martin Bormann and the Nazi party wanted was for anybody to know that Hitler had escaped. They wanted it to be as much a secret as the OSS or CIA wanted it to be because that would change everything. That would bring so many difficult things, especially for the United States. It was better for the body to be destroyed and cremated and the ashes distributed.

I don't think anybody wanted there to be a shrine to Adolph Hitler. It would raise far too many questions as to how he got away. And he would not have gotten away without the help of Allen Dulles of the OSS and various members of what became known as the Military-Industrial Complex in the United States, who benefitted hugely from the technology that the Nazis left behind.

The Office of Strategic Services OSS was a wartime intelligence agency of the United States during World War II and a predecessor to the Department of State's Bureau of Intelligence and Research and the Central Intelligence Agency.[8]

The military-industrial complex (MIC) is an informal alliance between a nation's military and the defense industry that supplies it, seen together as a vested interest that influences public policy.

A driving factor behind this relationship between the government and defense-minded corporations is that both sides benefit – one side from obtaining war weapons and the other from being paid to supply them. The term is most often used in reference to the system behind the military of the United States, where it is most prevalent due to close links between defense contractors, the

Pentagon, and politicians and gained popularity after a warning on its detrimental effects in the farewell address of President Dwight D. Eisenhower on January 17, 1961.[9]

Wernher von Braun is lauded as a great American hero, but not by me because he was a Nazi SS Colonel responsible for the deaths of about 30,000 forced laborers during World War II. Wernher von Braun was the man who put America on the Moon. Wernher von Braun and his Nazi scientists are the people who built NASA. Even multi tracking came out of the Nazis. So, there'd be no rock and roll if it hadn't been for the Nazis and their scientists.

Wernher Magnus Maximilian Freiherr von Braun was a German-born American aerospace engineer and space architect. He was the leading figure in the development of rocket technology in Nazi Germany and a pioneer of rocket and space technology in the United States. While in his twenties and early thirties, von Braun worked in

Nazi Germany's rocket development program. He helped design and develop the V-2 rocket at Peenemunde during World War II.[10] Following the war, he was secretly moved to the United States, along with about 1,600 other German scientists, engineers, and technicians, as part of Operation Paperclip. He worked for the United States Army on an intermediate-range ballistic missile program, and he developed the rockets that launched the United States' first space satellite Explorer 1.

In 1960, his group was assimilated into NASA, where he served as Director of the newly formed Marshall Space Flight Center and as the Chief Architect of the Saturn V super heavy-lift launch vehicle that propelled the Apollo spacecraft to the Moon. In 1967, von Braun was inducted into the National Academy of Engineering, and in 1975, he received the National Medal of Science.[11]

And we believe that all of this was part of a deal done between Martin Bormann and Dulles as the lead men, although John J. McCloy was also very involved at a later stage. A deal was made that the OSS would not just turn a blind eye, but it would help in return for all of this technology and the nuclear research that was going on and the scientists.

When these people were picked up by the allies after World War II, because of the confused Germany of 1945, where people were displaced all over the place and everything else, and yet we seem to know exactly where everybody is. We seem to know where all the treasure is, exactly where are the missile bases are. Somebody would have had to tell the allies where to go looking. Those instructions were followed very easily. We were picking things up because we knew where they were. Not because they were hidden successfully by the Nazis, or if they had been hidden, they told us where they were hiding them.

John Jay McCloy was an American lawyer, diplomat, banker, and Presidential Advisor. He served as Assistant Secretary of War during World

War II under Henry Stimson, helping deal with issues such as German sabotage, political tensions in the North Africa Campaign, and opposing the atomic bombings of Hiroshima and Nagasaki. After the war, he served as the President of the World Bank, U.S. High Commissioner for Germany, Chairman of Chase Manhattan Bank, Chairman of the Council on Foreign Relations, a member of the Warren Commission, and a prominent United States Adviser to all presidents from Franklin D. Roosevelt to Ronald Reagan.[12]

Allen Welsh Dulles was the first civilian Director of Central Intelligence and its longest-serving Director to date. As head of the Central Intelligence Agency (CIA) during the early Cold War, he oversaw the 1953 Iranian coup d'état, the 1954 Guatemalan coup d'état, the Lockheed U-2 aircraft program, the Project MKUltra mind control program, and the Bay of Pigs Invasion. He was fired by John F. Kennedy over the latter fiasco. Dulles was one of the members of the Warren Commission investigating the assassination of John F. Kennedy. Between his stints of government service, Dulles was a corporate lawyer and partner at Sullivan & Cromwell.[13]

In return, Adolf Hitler, Marin Bormann, and up to 100,000 European fascists escaped, many of them with the collusion of the Catholic Church by their side, to Argentina and other places in Latin America. Also, to Egypt, where they helped the Egyptians build their rocket. Syria as well and Turkey, both of which were pro-fascist.

Q. It's really about the money, isn't it?

A. Everything is about the money.

Q. I mean, there were about 300 American companies supplying Germany while they were bombing Britain, correct?

A. Yes, actively helping the Nazis. The Ford Motor Company made something like a third of the vehicles that the German army and military used. So, that's German vehicles taking German soldiers to the beaches of Normandy, where the American soldiers in Ford Motor vehicles are coming ashore to be killed and kill Germans.

At the same time, all the money is going back to "Motor City" Detroit and into the pockets of the Ford Motor Company. GM was also heavily involved in supplying the Reich with material plans and engineering.

IBM was heavily involved in the Holocaust. ITT was making Focke-Wulf fighters, which were shooting down American bombers over Europe.

It was all about money. The thing that made me very cynical now is that you can see the same things being played out nowadays. You can see it being played out in Iraq, where people are making billions while our young boys are dying on the ground.

I don't believe in the Illuminati, Skull and Bones, or any other secret society running the world, but it is run by a select bunch of people who get together at various stages and decide on how to make money.

Q. You were mentioning the church earlier. There have always been rumors of the Catholic Church helping Nazis escape. So, what was their involvement?

A. I don't think it. There are huge documents of evidence to show that Pope Pius knew. One of his cardinals, who was a Croatian fascist, anyway, was the guy who actually ran the operation. That's detailed in *Grey Wolf*. We've had a lot more detail since then, and some very brave writers published books about the church's involvement with the Nazis before, during, and after the war.

I think that there was a section in the Catholic church that saw these people as "Teutonic Warriors for Christ," and that's a strange thing for us from this historical distance to look at. They were Jew-killers. They killed Jews, and the Jews were Christ-killers. They had fought against the Soviet Union, which was completely and totally godless in Communism. As such, it would be seen by some people within the church as being brave, not criminal.

"Teutonic warriors" or the Teutonic Order was formed to aid Christians on their pilgrimages to the Holy Land and to establish hospitals. Its members have commonly been known as the "Teutonic Knights," having a small voluntary and mercenary military membership, serving as a crusading military order for the protection of Christians in the Holy Land and the Baltic during the Middle Ages.[14]

So, the Vatican, along with the International Committee to the Red Cross and the two Swiss Diplomats, handed these people travel papers, and in many cases, money to get out. In the period between 1945 and '48, over 100,000 got out through the Vatican. They weren't just German Nazis; there were Belgian Nazis; there were French Nazis and Scandinavian Nazis.

The whole of the Croatian Ustase fascists got out by the Vatican with their gold. I don't know if you've ever been to Vatican City, but it's very small. It's only about a mile in total. To get 100,000 men of a certain age through there without anybody noticing is impossible.

The Ustaše was a Croatian fascist, ultranationalist, and terrorist organization, which was active, as one organization, between 1929 and 1945. Its members murdered hundreds of thousands of Serbs, Jews, and Roma, as well as political dissidents in Yugoslavia during World War II. They were known for their particularly brutal and sadistic methods of execution, which often included torture and dismemberment.[15] Much of the ideology of the Ustaše was based on Nazi racial theory. Like the Nazis, the Ustaše deemed Jews, Romani, and Slavs to be sub-humans. They endorsed the claims from German racial theorists that Croats were not Slavs but a Germanic race.[16]

Q. How did Hitler get to Argentina? What was the physical route he took?

A. At midnight on May 27, 1945, they walked out of the bunker and into his personal quarters of the Reich Chancellery, the new Reich Chancellery, where behind a sliding partition on the wall of his bedroom, there was a tunnel down to an underground bunker.

Our understanding is that in that underground bunker were waiting two look-a-likes for them, who were later transferred into the bunker and executed. Hitler, Eva Braun, her brother-in-law Hermann Fegelein, and a group of SS commandos would have taken them down further into the underground system in Berlin.

That door is supposed to still be there, but we can't get permission to go and see it, funnily enough. They would have walked through the underground up onto a cleared roadway.

Waiting for them was a Ju 52 piloted by Captain Peter Baumgart. Baumgart then flew them to Tander in Denmark, which used to be the imperial Zeppelin base. They then boarded a Ju 252, which is a pressurized and much bigger aircraft capable of flying at 30,000 feet, and that got them down very close to Barcelona.

They again changed planes and flew to the island of Fuerteventura, Canary Islands. They were then met by three submarines from the last wolf pack from the war, interesting enough called "Seawolf."

Fifty-three days later, after what could not have been a comfortable submerged voyage over, they were landed on the coast of Argentina.

Q. So, the pilot that flew Hitler actually reported it to authorities?

A. Yes. In 1947, he was in a Warsaw court where he was accused of being a member of the SS, and there was another pilot, Peter Baumgart, who was SS at Auschwitz, but not this guy. He told them that he was a pilot and he flew Adolf Hitler, along with Eva Braun. He gave details of the flight, how it happened, who he was carrying, and what happened when they got on the ground in Tander.

All of that was reported by Reuters, the Associated Press, UPI, and there are pieces in newspapers all over the world in 1947, saying this guy flew Hitler out.

We also have the testimony of the SS officer who was wounded on the ground at Tander. He saw Hitler alive and heard him give a final speech to the men there.

We then have over a dozen witnesses in Argentina who saw Hitler and Eva at various stages in the 1950s.

So, none of these things were made up by us. This stuff is sourced.

Q. Who was killed in the bunker then?

A. We sent a lot of pictures that are supposed to be the last ones of Adolf Hitler to a very senior facial recognition expert in London, who works a lot for the Metropolitan Police, and asked him if this was Adolf Hitler. We gave him pictures that we knew were of Hitler to compare.

So, the last picture of Adolf Hitler that everybody has seen is a man giving medals to a group of young Hitler youth who had been Soviet tank-killing is definitely not Adolf Hitler. We believe he's the man who was executed in the bunker and his body taken upstairs.

It wouldn't have been very difficult to find a look-a-like for Eva Braun. Goebbels' had a whole stable of actresses that he could have called on to replace her. She wasn't known well by anybody except for what they referred to as the mountain people. So, it would have only been the senior high command – not even the high command in the military, but people like Himmler, Goebbels, but not anybody else.

Heinrich Luitpold Himmler was Reichsführer of the Schutzstaffel and a leading member of the Nazi Party of Germany. Himmler was one of the most powerful men in Nazi Germany and a main architect of the Holocaust. As a member of a reserve battalion during World War I, Himmler did not see active service.

Paul Joseph Goebbels was a German Nazi politician and Reich Minister of Propaganda of Nazi Germany from 1933 to 1945. He was one of Adolf Hitler's closest and most devoted associates and was known for his skills in public speaking and his deeply virulent antisemitism, which was evident in his publicly voiced views.[17]

Q. What about the skull that the Russians recently found?

A. It's a skull of a woman who was in her forties, so it couldn't even have been Eva Braun, and that was tested by a DNA expert from the states. His results were pretty conclusive. The Russian's FSB, the successors to the KGB, says, "No, it isn't. It's Adolf Hitler." But they won't release it for independent DNA testing.

The only thing that's made up is Hugh Trevor-Roper's *Last days of Adolf Hitler*, and why he wrote that lie, I don't know. Well, I do have an idea. I think that those in power in the Allied community wanted a full stop – a period with a line drawn underneath it.

So that they could say, "We won. It's over. We killed him."

Hugh Redwald Trevor-Roper, Baron Dacre of Glanton, was an English historian. He was Regius Professor of Modern History at the University of Oxford. Trevor-Roper was a polemicist and essayist on a range of historical topics, but particularly England in the 16th and 17th centuries and Nazi Germany.

Trevor-Roper's most widely read and financially rewarding book was titled *The Last Days of Hitler* in 1947. It emerged from his assignment as a British intelligence officer in 1945 to discover what happened in the last days of Hitler's bunker. From his interviews with a range of witnesses and study of surviving documents, he demonstrated that Hitler was dead and had not escaped from Berlin. He also showed that Hitler's dictatorship was not an efficient unified machine but a hodge-podge of overlapping rivalries. Trevor-Roper's reputation was "severely damaged" in 1983 when he authenticated the *Hitler Diaries* shortly before they were shown to be forgeries.[18]

Q. What was Hitler's life like in Argentina? Because by 1945, wasn't he the wealthiest man in Europe?

A. Well, the party, was the wealthiest operation in Europe. Martin Bormann controlled all of the money, but he would have lived a comfortable life. I've been to the house where he spent some time, which is beautiful on the shore of a gorgeous lake overlooking the Andes.

It looks very much like Bavaria. In fact, the whole area is very Bavarian. German is spoken a great deal there. There are many German families down there, German schools, and micro-breweries that make German beer. All the state agencies were in Spanish and German. You can wake up there, look out, and think you are in Germany.

But I think he had a very quiet life. I don't think he was very well. We have the notes of his personal doctor in Argentina. He seems to have had a trembling problem in his hands, which was probably the result of scarlet fever he caught after World War 1. The wounds in his face from the bomb, the July bomb plot, were probably a lot worse than people thought they were. I know that he had to have another operation on his face because he had problems breathing. He also had a heart condition.

So, I think he lived a quiet middle-class life. They would go to Buenos Ares a number of times to meet with other senior Nazis. We have eyewitness accounts of them doing just that. But it seems that Bormann kept his very isolated when it really came down to it because he didn't want them to know Hitler was alive. He felt that brand had been busted.

Q. What did he die of? Old age?

A. Heart attack, it looks like, some sort of coronary problem. It seems that he had a couple of strokes, and then he just went out with a heart attack quietly in his sleep.

Q. What happened to the Nazi party? I'm guessing that they would have had to change in order to survive.

A. Yes, I think so. If they had spent the sort of money they spent on the "Final Solution" on fighting World War II, they would have won. I think Bormann and his compatriots in the German industry and the American industry all realized that there was a far better way to obtain power. You just use money. You don a major brand with a swastika for people to march behind. All you need to control is the method of production. By that, you can control the people, and if you control the people, then you've got them.

The "Final Solution" was a Nazi plan for the genocide of Jews during World War II. The "Final Solution to the Jewish question" was the official code name for the murder of all Jews within reach, which was not restricted to the European continent. This policy of deliberate and systematic genocide starting across German-occupied Europe was formulated in procedural and geopolitical terms by Nazi leadership in January 1942 at the Wannsee Conference held near Berlin and culminated in the Holocaust, which saw the killing of 90% of Polish Jews and two-thirds of the Jewish population of Europe.[19]

They would have come to terms with the fact that there was no point in trying to destroy the Jewish race. It would have been a complete waste of time. I think, during the war, they were a criminal gang. But after it, they became a serious business with links to all major international companies and links to international banking.

They rebuilt West Germany after the war and then absorbed East Germany after the wall came down. And it's been a success. It's been far more of a success than the British story after World War II or of France. Germany is the dominant power in Europe. It can tell Greece, Italy, Portugal, and Spain what to do. They don't have to do that with attacks anymore. They do it by handling their banknotes.

Q. Where is the Nazi party today?

A. It still exists at the board-level across major German companies. All of their descendants control the holdings. I don't think politically it does. It's probably been absorbed into lots of other parties. I don't think there's one single Nazi party left. It's a different thing now compared to the way it was in the 1940s. But the control of the money, control of the economy, is still in the hands of the descendants of the people who stole it in the first place.

Q. Whatever happened to Hitler's descendants?

A. The two girls seemed to have disappeared in Argentina. It would have been pretty simple. They were pretty wealthy. They could change their names, and they could travel anywhere. They could be living in New York and London now. They could even be back in Berlin.

I don't know if they had families. I know that the elder of the two girls didn't have any children from an interview she gave to a divorce lawyer in Buenos Ares. But I'm not sure about the other girl. I don't even know her name. It's also one of those things that I don't do. I'm not chasing children. The sins of the father should not be visited on the sons or daughters, in this case.

Q. Didn't Hitler have some relatives that moved to New York at one time?

A. There were two, maybe three, first cousins that were living in Manhattan, who were given lives after the war by the U.S. government. On the grounds that they never had children, and they kept to that. He had second and third cousins, I think, in Germany and Austria. But nobody close. He did have a sister named Paula, but she died post-war as well. I think she's buried up at the Eagle's Nest.

Q. So, they were trying to control the birth line?

A. Yes. You never want an heir for something you really don't like. I mean, I don't know what will happen to Osama Bin Laden's children. He seemed to have a lot of them. But in Hitler's case, apart from the two girls, again, I don't know if the second girl had a family; there's no bloodline left.

Q. Were the FBI ever trying to find Hitler?

A. The FBI files make for interesting reading. There's a lot of junk in there, but it seems pretty obvious that Hoover believed he had escaped. He took reports seriously of Hitler being in Argentina. There are some interesting, with heavily redacted material, in there. It makes it difficult to further the research.

The CIA doesn't release anything. We've tried Freedom of Information, but it doesn't work. The same thing is true in Great Britain. The material keeps getting stamped for fifty years, as it's necessary for the defense of national security. I think it'll be a long-time before all the information comes out.

Q. Whatever happened to Bormann?

A. I think he probably died sometime in the 1980s, in Argentina, in Buenos Ares, in a big villa. It's not been something we followed up on. We have a follow up to *Grey Wolf* called *The Spider's Web*, which we've been looking for a publisher for. Our original publisher in the United States, which is part of the Barnes & Noble group, is stalling. They are too scared to publish it.

Q. What about the leaders of Argentina, Eva Perón, and her husband? Were they Nazis as well?

A. Yes, they've been in the pay of the Nazis since 1941. The story that is told in Evita is a load of rubbish. They knew each other well before that. Yes, but both were paid by the Nazi party.

There is a brilliant Argentine Senator that got all of the check-book stubs and everything else and wrote a book called *A Tradition of Treason*, which details the Peróns' involvement with the Nazis pre-war and post-war. The Nazi party funded the actual coup that brought the Colonel into power in Argentina. This was a fascist dictatorship, not what people in Argentina who still think Perón was a God.

María Eva Duarte, better known as Eva Perón and Evita, was the wife of Argentine President Juan Perón was the First Lady of Argentina from 1946 until her death in 1952. In 1934, at the age of 15, she moved to the nation's capital of Buenos Aires to pursue a career as a stage, radio, and film actress. She met Colonel Juan Perón on January 22, 1944, during a charity event at the Luna Park Stadium to benefit the victims of an earthquake in San Juan, Argentina. The two were married the following year.[20]

Juan Perón was elected President of Argentina in 1946, and during the next six years, Eva Perón became powerful within the pro-Peronist trade unions, primarily for speaking on behalf of labor rights. She also ran the Ministries of Labor and Health, founded and ran the charitable Eva Perón Foundation, championed women's suffrage in Argentina, and founded and ran the nation's first large-scale female political party, the Female Peronist Party.[21]

After World War II, Argentina became a haven for Nazi war criminals, with explicit protection from Perón.[22] Examples of Nazis and collaborators who relocated to Argentina include Emile Dewoitine, who arrived in May 1946 and worked on the Pulqui jet; Erich Priebke, who arrived in 1947; Josef Mengele in 1949; Adolf Eichmann in 1950; Austrian representative of the Škoda arms manufacturer in Spain Reinhard Spitzy; Charles Lescat, editor of Je Suis Partout in Vichy France; SS functionary Ludwig Lienhardt; and SS-Hauptsturmführer Klaus Barbie.[23]

The German-Argentine community in Argentina is the fourth-largest immigrant group in the country, after the ethnic Spanish and the Italians. The German-Argentine community predated Juan Perón's presidency and began during the political unrest related to the 19th-century unification of Germany.

While Juan Perón's Argentina allowed many Nazi criminals to take refuge in the country following World War II, the society also accepted more Jewish immigrants than any other country in Latin America. Today, Argentina has a population of more than 200,000 Jewish citizens, the largest in Latin America, the third-largest in the Americas, and the sixth-largest in the world.[24]

Listen to the full interview with Gerrard Williams on my website:

www.alanrwarren.com/hom-podcast-episodes/episode/a95ee6ce/hunting-hitler-gerrard-williams-encore-2014

Interview Afterthoughts

The "Hitler Escaped the Bunker Theory" is really like the granddaddy to conspiracy theories. In fact, it's so old and ingrained in society that it's more like part of history. I remember being a kid in the 60s and hearing many stories about Hitler still being alive. This is probably why I wanted to interview people on the subject – to try and separate what my impressionable young mind believed and what facts are out there.

The recent surge in conspiracies since the turn of the century also created popularity in Hitler. So much so, the History Channel decided to run a series on it, and I believe there were three seasons, so people must have watched. The series got terrible reviews, though. That's probably because most of the hosts and players in the series were not qualified.

There was a time once when television networks like History, Discovery, and even A&E were places you could go to find the truth about things that occurred in the world around us. These days, it's more about ratings and getting popular or good-looking hosts on to attract an audience. This was definitely the case with the *Hitler Series* on History. Season One had a couple of qualified people working on it, but by Season Two, it turned into another reality show with lots of drama about things that had nothing to do with the case.

I respect Bob Baer, who was an American CIA agent and author, though when we see him on these kinds of series, he's just in the headquarters giving directions and not really out in the field investigating. It almost feels like he's just there to give the show some credibility.

The only other member that I respected for any kind of journalism was Gerrard Williams – a longtime reporter for several large media organizations. This is why only his interviews are included in this book. I felt I was getting real "from the heart" answers from him and nothing more.

Do I think Hitler actually escaped from the bunker? I'm on the fence because there's definitely proof of the Peróns being Nazis and very involved with the party, as well as a large amount of the population being Nazis. So, it's logical to believe it would be the landing place for Hitler as it was for so many other wanted Nazis after the war.

But all that has really been proven by Williams or any others involved in this case is that there was a way for Hitler to escape. The underground tunnels, Hitler look-a-likes, the German submarine base, and the pilot who claimed he flew Hitler and Eva Braun to Denmark. But there is no hard evidence presented by anybody to this day. I realize that something that happened so many years ago does create the problem of getting any hard evidence from anywhere and will probably remain a mystery forever.

But, is it possible? Yes.

---

1. Grey Wolf: The Escape of Adolf Hitler - Wikipedia. https://en.wikipedia.org/wiki/ Grey_Wolf:_The_Escape_of_Adolf_Hitler
2. Hunting Hitler | History TV South Africa. https://www. historytv.africa/shows/hunting-hitler-0
3. Georgy Zhukov - Wikipedia. https://en.wikipedia.org/ wiki/Georgy_K._Zhukov
4. History You Didn't Know About - OP Paperclip | The .... https://thesupernaturalbiblechanges.com/blog/history-you-didn-t-know-about-op-paperclip
5. History of Martin Bormann - Timeline - Historydraft. https://historydraft.com/story/martin-bormann/timeline/407
6. Martin Bormann Explained. http://everything.explained.today/Martin_Bormann/
7. Martin Bormann - Wikipedia. https://en.wikipedia.org/wiki/Martin_Borman
8. Office of the Coordinator of Information - WikiMili, The .... https://wikimili.com/en/Office_of_the_Coordinator_of_Information
9. Military industrial complex - Pathway to Prosperity .... https://pathwaytoprosperity.com/glossary/military-industrial-complex/
10. Wernher von Braun: "I have learned to use the word http://quodid.com/quotes/12142/wernher-von-braun/i-have-learned-to-use-the-word-impossible

11. Wernher von Braun — Google Arts & Culture. https://artsandculture.google.com/entity/wernher-von-braun/m0850x

12. John J. McCloy - Wikipedia. https://en.wikipedia.org/wiki/John_J._McCloy

13. Allen Dulles - Wikipedia. https://en.wikipedia.org/wiki/Allen_Dulles

14. Teutonic Order - Wikipedia. https://en.wikipedia.org/wiki/Teutonic_Order

15. History of the Jews in Bosnia and Herzegovina - WikiMili .... https://wikimili.com/en/History_of_the_Jews_in_Bosnia_and_Herzegovina

16. Ustaše - Wikipedia. https://en.wikipedia.org/wiki/Ustasi

17. Joseph Goebbels — Google Arts & Culture. https://artsandculture.google.com/entity/joseph-goebbels/m040by

18. The Greatest Books: Written by Hugh Trevor-Roper. https://thegreatestbooks.org/authors/6926

19. Final Solution — Google Arts & Culture. https://artsandculture.google.com/entity/m02rr1

20. Eva Perón — Google Arts & Culture. https://artsandculture.google.com/entity/m0dltj

21. Eva Perón - Wikipedia. https://en.wikipedia.org/wiki/Eva_Duarte_de_Per%C3%B3n

22. Juan Perón | Military Wiki | Fandom. https://military.wikia.org/wiki/Juan_Per%C3%B3n

23. Juan Perón - Wikipedia. https://en.wikipedia.org/wiki/Juan_Per%C3%B3n

24. Secret Base in Chile - Page 2 - Axis History Forum. https://forum.axishistory.com/viewtopic.php?t=227424&start=15

911 Attack

The Conspiracy Theory

"911" are the three numbers that everybody easily recognizes in the 21st century. Such a disastrous event that seemed to pull the American people together and act as one soon dissipated over the last twenty years. It goes hand in hand with the current distrust of the government, where its citizens no longer believe what they are told. They believe that in the last ten years, everything bad that has ever happened was caused by one or all of the government agencies.

I have to say that the hardest part about trying to find out if a conspiracy has any merit is the researching of the conspiracy claimers. When something occurs, such as the 911 Twin Tower attack on New York City, the stories run wild. So, now it's essential to research each theory and look for any real evidence behind it. If you find someone with some piece of information that looks credible, then it's key to talk with them.

Interview with Rebekah Roth

One of the best examples I can show you is Rebekah Roth, a person who wrote *Methodical Illusion* in November of 2014. From what I had heard at the time, she seemed very credible and wasn't raving in a weird way on any of the shows I had heard her on. Well, at least not to that point. But that changed, and she exposed herself as being a quack. Even conspiracy nut, Jim Marrs, called her out publicly! Believe me; you would have to do something pretty insane to get Marrs calling you a conspiracy quack.

Below are the highlights, or lowlights, depending on how you feel about the 911 conspiracy theories. Roth had at least three more books covering the same topic after this book. This interview took place in early 2015, and I was working out of the KKNW 1150 A.M. studios in Seattle.

Rebekah Roth had a nearly thirty-year airline career working as both a flight attendant and an international purser. She was trained as an emergency medical technician and served as a volunteer firefighter. Her expertise and training as a flight attendant allowed her to research the events of September 11, 2001, with an insider's knowledge that eventually lead her to discover details and answers to some of the most haunting questions surrounding that infamous day in our history.[1]

Q. Tell the listeners who you are and what you did that led you to write this book?

A. Sure. I was a flight attendant for about 30 years, and I retired in 2004. Everybody said to me, "You ought to write a book." But I never did. Somewhere around 2008 or '09, I thought, I am going to write a book about what that life was like because it's kind of mysterious life.

A lot of people don't know what we do. I remember before I got hired as a flight attendant, I always wondered what a flight attendant did after we got off the plane. So, I started to write this book. At the very first, I wanted to introduce a Middle-eastern character, and I just wanted the name of a character. I usually just go to a book of baby names I have, but it didn't have any Middle-eastern names in there. I wanted this person to be an Arabic-type.

So, I just thought that I would Google search those 911 hijackers and grab the first name from one and the last name from another. Up in front of me came a BBC article dated September 23, 2001, and it told me that the Saudi government was suing the FBI for stealing the identity and claiming that six of their citizens were being falsely accused of being 911 hijackers.

They were still alive, and a couple of them had actually been airline pilots. I followed this really close. I watched it unfold on television that day, and I watched it straight for ten days. My schedule allowed me to be in front of my TV for the first ten days.

There were some strange things I was seeing unfold. But I had never heard of Al-Qaeda, and I'd never heard of Osama Bin Laden as being a threat to our airline, or to any airline, or to our country. In our yearly training, which I had just had, we studied potential hijackers every year. So that we would know what they looked like, who they were, and what their agenda might be, or where they might want to go.

Al-Qaeda operates as a network of Islamic extremists and Salafist jihadists. The organization has been designated as a terrorist group by the United Nations Security Council, the North Atlantic Treaty Organization (NATO), the European Union, the United States, China, the United Kingdom, Russia, India, and various other countries. Al-Qaeda has mounted attacks on non-military and military targets in various countries, including the 1998 United States embassy bombings, the September 11 attacks, and the 2002 Bali bombings.[2]

Q. So, that would be quite unusual that they didn't mention it in your training?

A. Yes, especially when I saw what they did. They somehow commandeered Norad and made it, so the six-minute response time was an hour and a half. Where was our air force? Where was our fighter jets? When I was watching, I thought we were just going to scramble fighter jets and take care of the hijackers, but nothing happened.

So, I thought those guys must have been really good. Not just to hijack one airplane but four, and to make it, so our response system fell apart the way it did. Nobody could even understand if these planes were being hijacked or not. So, I had always known that there was something wrong.

When I read this BBC article, I thought, "Hey, wait a minute." Now, I saw what they wanted us to believe. I saw the second plane crash into the tower, and that's exactly when I turned my television on. At that moment. So, how could these six guys be alive?

The fact that the FBI was being sued by the Saudi Government over these six citizens of theirs and a couple of them had never visited the United States. And they used their passport photos and their home addresses.

Q. So, they have never resolved that case?

A. Not as far as I can find out. In fact, ten of the accused hijackers of the 911 event are still alive. That's when I put my novel on hold and started looking into the 911 event. I couldn't believe what I saw.

I'd actually had jets scrambled for an incident onboard, and it does take about six minutes. It's hair-raising to be there, but you do get this feeling of safety. To realize that our protection, our jets were never scrambled that day. It took them over an hour-and-a-half to even show up, and by then, it already happened.

I remember that day looking back. There were no plane parts at a crash site in Shanksville. When I saw the Pentagon got hit, I heard CNN say, "There's no plane crash here. There's no plane." I know that planes don't disappear into buildings, and yet the official story was that it was a plane.

I've flown a lot of 757s, and I know how big that plane is, and there were no parts there, no tail section, or anything. So, my mission was to find the planes, passengers, and crews. To find out what happened that day on those four passenger jets.

Q. Was it hard to get the information from the FBI and other agencies?

A. Most of it is found online. Get your Google on. If you want to read a hard print of the Official 911 Commission hearings, it has been published online in a PDF format. I also went away from what we often refer to as the mainstream media. I used their information as well and read as much stuff that came out in those first ten days. I remember thinking about how fast CNN was getting passenger manifests and names of passengers, and it was uncanny to me how fast information about the passengers came out.

Q. That's unusual?

A. Very unusual. Airline corporations are very large companies, and we do have some standards. Typically, what would happen is that they have a group of people that would start contacting the next of kin for all of the passengers, and information would not be given to the media or even to the FBI until the next of kin is notified.

Q. There have been several things said about the many phone calls that came from those planes. What did you find out about any of them that got your attention?

A. I took the phone calls one-by-one and methodically went through them. Since I was a flight attendant for so long and a purser, I put my old flight attendant shoes on, and I started with Flight 11.

On Flight 11, two flight attendants called out from that plane. There were almost 100 people between the crew and passengers on the flight that day, yet only two people called out.

We were told the official story by the government that one girl, Amy Sweeny, called her supervisor, and according to the supervisor, she called on her cell phone. Well, I knew that it was an impossibility to do that from that altitude. The FBI tried to change that later on to be an air-phone, but that isn't much better than a cell phone. One of the reasons why Boeing 757 didn't have an air-phone on was that they were so ineffective, and oftentimes, we found they were so poorly. Maybe if you used one phone in first-class or one in coach, but if you had somebody on the phone in first-class, oftentimes that second phone couldn't even connect. They were very expensive, and their quality was not very good. So, oftentimes, you would pay $13 a minute for just static, or your call would drop. So, they were not much better than trying to use a cell phone.

A cell phone was impossible at that altitude. I actually have done experiments around that same time of 2000 or 2001 standing in the back galley of a 757 with a bunch of other flight attendants. At that time, we all had our little Nokia phones, and some had those high-tech flip-open phones.

The aircraft itself was made of aluminum and wiring in there, and we were back by the tail section. It was like a Faraday cage, so oftentimes, maybe the T-Mobile person or the Sprint person wouldn't have any bars, or they'd barely have a bar or two, and maybe the AT&T or the Verizon person would have three. We were often weakened at a major airport, and that was just sitting on the ground. So, I'm telling you that cell phones wouldn't work in the air.

There were two flight attendants that called in at the exact same minute, and that was at about 20 minutes after they left Boston. I've flown out of Boston, so I have a pretty good idea where the territory was where they were actually located. Betty Ong was the first flight attendant. She called reservations, which was a very unusual place for any employee to call because you are always on hold for 20 minutes. In an emergency, as a hijacking would be, I thought that was the craziest number you would call. You could call your supervisor or someone else, but reservations isn't easy for us to get through either. Since then, I've been contacted by lots of flight attendants that knew these girls. They said that always struck them as being really weird too. We didn't have a hotline directly from our airplanes to where somebody would pick up immediately.

So, Betty Ong calls into the reservations line, and the first thing Betty Ong says is, I couldn't even believe what I was reading, she said, "He," as in one hijacker, not the five or four that the government said, "He has sprayed pepper spray, or mace, or something in business class and we can't breathe in business class." She tells the reservation's gal that she's seated at 3R, which is about 150 feet from business class. So, it's kind of a long distance.

However, let me just give you an inside track. If you are in a pressurized aircraft at the altitude they were supposed to be, and someone sprays cheap perfume, mace, pepper spray, or something else inside that cabin, and even if you remember the days when we had smoking onboard the front half, everyone smelled the smoke. Well, it's the same kind of thing with pepper spray or mace. Within two to three minutes, everyone on the aircraft, including the hijackers, the pilots, the crew members, and all the passengers, would be suffering from the effects of the mace.

Yet, she sat on the phone for 20 minutes and never coughed or complained about the pepper spray or mace. I realized right then and there that that aircraft was no longer pressurized. Then, she went on to say something else that maybe only a flight attendant maybe could hear. She said, "He stood upstairs," and there are no stairs on a 767. There are only stairs on the 747. She's on a 767 where there are no stairs.

American Airlines Flight 11 was the first hijacked airplane of the September 11 attacks. It crashed into the North Tower of the World Trade Center. The American Airlines airplane was a Boeing 767. It was scheduled to fly from Logan International Airport in Boston to Los Angeles International Airport. Fifteen minutes after takeoff, the hijackers forced their way into the cockpit.[3]

The 767 features a twin-aisle cabin with a typical configuration of six abreast in business class and seven across in economy. The standard seven abreast, 2–3–2 economy class layout places approximately 87 percent of all seats at a window or aisle.[4]

But there are stairs in a hanger, every hanger because hangers are real tall buildings, and the bigger the airplane, the taller the building. That level is usually filled with office space up there. There are oftentimes stairs there in every corner of a large hanger.

She then says, "We're the first." And they were the first. Flight 11 was the first plane that we were told that hit the North Tower. The very first event of that day. I thought, how would she have known that they were going to be the first if someone hadn't told her?

Then, it started to look to me that they were actually on the ground – no longer pressurized or she would have been suffering from the mace or pepper spray, and that they were in a hanger, where there were stairs and where the hijacker stood at or stood up. Then, when she said that they were the first, I realized that someone had told her the scenario of the day. She had been briefed by someone on what possibly was presented to them as a drill. Then, I continued to look into these two flight attendants' words very carefully.

At this point, I realized nobody else had heard their words with the ears of a flight attendant. She was being told the scenario of the day by what she had just said. She also said, "We're up in the air." And then she said, "I don't know, but we might be being hijacked."

I thought that's odd as a hijacking only takes place up in the air. No flight attendant would have to explain that they were up in the air unless someone was telling her that she better convince whoever she was talking to that they were in the air or that the scenario was that she was calling from the plane. If the hijacking took place on the ground, we would open the doors and get the passengers out. So, her saying that they were in the air was her trying to convince the person on the other end of the phone call that they were, in fact, in the air.

Betty Ann Ong was an American flight attendant aboard American Airlines Flight 11, the first airplane to become hijacked during the September 11 attacks. Shortly after the hijacking, Ong notified the American Airlines ground crew of the hijacking, staying on the telephone for 25 minutes and relaying vital information that eventually led to the closing of airspace by the FAA for the first time in United States history. On September 11, 2001, Ong assigned herself to

Flight 11, so she could return to Los Angeles and go on vacation to Hawaii with her sister. During the hijacking, she used a telephone card to call American Airlines' operations/Raleigh reservations center from the plane's rear galley.[5]

I went from her to Amy Sweeney. Amy Sweeney was the other flight attendant that called in. She called her supervisor in Boston that she had just checked out with that morning. She told him that the hijacker was in 9B. Again, she referred to the hijacker as one person, a "he." Unlike the official story, I read the official story.

Madeline "Amy" Sweeney was Born on December 14, 1965, in Valley Stream, NY. Amy left behind her husband, Michael, and her two young children when she died as Flight 11 hit the North Tower. Amy is widely believed to have been the female flight attendant Betty communicated with during her call with Gonzalez. In fact, Amy made her own call to American Airlines Flight Service at Logan airport. She made the call from a passenger seat in the next-to-last passenger row in the coach cabin using an air-phone. After her first call was disconnected after a short time, she made another attempt to call in. At that time, she was connected to American Airlines flight service manager and her personal friend of over a decade, Michael Woodward.[6]

Then, she called back to her supervisor and said, "I made a mistake." No flight attendant would ever make that mistake. In a hijacking, we have set protocols, and at the time of 911, they were called the "Common Strategy" set up by the FAA from the '70s. That common strategy was steps, procedures, and code words that we were to follow step-by-step. What I was seeing with these two flight attendants is neither one of them was really following the steps.

In a hijacking, what we would do is coordinate if we were talking to someone on the ground, or the pilots talk to somebody on the ground, once they found out that they were being hijacked. There was a set of protocols to follow.

Once we got on the ground, some sort of liberation force like a Delta Force, Navy Seals, FBI, somebody would come and storm the aircraft and rescue the hostages or the passengers and crew from the hijacker.

If I told them through the pilots or somebody I was talking to on the ground that the hijacker was in 9B, and he really wasn't a hijacker, that guy could potentially be killed innocently. And it's a mistake no flight attendant would ever have made.

So, when she called back saying that she had made a mistake, she said, "9B has actually been stabbed, and the hijackers are in 10 A and B. So, the hijackers were right behind him." Well, I did a little research on who the passenger was in 9B, and lo and behold, was I shocked to hear this, he was a highly-trained assassin for a foreign government. He was also trained in anti-hijacking procedures and in hostage rescue. Hostage rescue is who would come and liberated the plane. Here he was on-board.

Sayeret Matkal, meaning Sayeret (special reconnaissance unit) of the Matkal (General Staff), is the prime sayeret unit of the Israel Defense Forces. First and foremost, a field intelligence-gathering unit, conducting deep reconnaissance behind enemy lines to obtain strategic intelligence, Sayeret Matkal is also tasked with counterterrorism and hostage rescue beyond Israel's borders.[7]

He was actually with the Israeli defense forces special operations unit, called Sayeret Matkal. He was fluent in English as he grew up in Denver, Colorado. He was fluent in Arabic and Hebrew. So, we are expected to believe that a trained assassin and an anti-hijacking specialist, fluent in the language spoken by the hijackers, was sitting in the row behind him.

Think about this for a minute. The last time you flew and you overheard the people talking behind you. Sometimes we hear embarrassing conversations or arguments even because it's really easy when they're less than two-feet behind us. To hear planning of what was referred to as the "New Pearl Harbor," and he did nothing. And then, on their way to the cockpit to commandeer it, these two five-feet-six and five-foot-seven hijackers decided they would stab him with a plastic boxcutter and kill him. His friends said that he could kill any human being with a pen and a credit card. That's when it hit me. It wasn't hijackers on-board. It was handlers.

Daniel Mark Lewin – 31-years old, sometimes spelled Levin, was an American Israeli mathematician and entrepreneur who co-founded internet company Akamai Technologies. Lewin served for four years in the Israel Defense Forces (IDF) as an officer in Sayeret Matkal, one of the IDF's special forces units. Lewin earned the rank of Captain. Lewin was on the American Airlines Flight 11 and in seat 9B as it was hijacked during the September 11 attacks. According to the 9/11

Commission, Lewin was stabbed by one of the hijackers, probably Satam al-Suqami, who was seated directly behind him after attempting to foil the hijacking.[8]

I continued to look at the other flight attendant, Amy Sweeney, and what information she was giving to the company through her supervisor after she made the mistake that no flight attendant would ever make of labeling an innocent person as a terrorist or hijacker. She also said that 9B was being attended to by a doctor and a nurse. She said that Betty Ong was seated with her in the second to the last row in coach. Again, they are about 150-feet away from the cockpit, first-class business-class, the first part of the aircraft. So, it's very hard to know what's going on up there. According to Amy Sweeney, they were sitting together in the second to the last row but remember that Betty Ong said about ten times that she was seated in her jump seat at 3R, which is quite a ways away from the last row in coach.

I see a very important problem here because it's quite important in a hijacking that you give the same information. It can't be two things because those girls are in two locations. Either in a coach seat together, or one is in a coach seat, and the other is in her jump seat.

Betty Ong said that they paged for a doctor and nobody showed up. So, we have someone saying that a doctor and a nurse are attending in 9B, and we have someone else saying that there's nobody to help him.

Q. What about the box cutter?

A. I actually found a picture of the box cutter that they claimed was used. They claimed it was one of the only things they found from Flight 93 in a ditch at Shanksville, Pennsylvania. No titanium engine parts, nothing but a plastic cutter showed up, along with a paper passport by one of the hijackers.

It's one of the bright plastic ones that you can find at Lowes or Home Depot. They are really cheap, and they break really easily.

They are serrated about every quarter-inch, and the blade is meant to break off. They are very frustrating to use, even on cardboard. Can you imagine decapitating someone with one?

If you really want to try and do what the government wants you to believe happened, go and buy a chicken and go to Lowes Hardware or Home Depot, and pick up one of those bright yellow, and these are not linoleum cutters, these are the plastic ones with handles about four or five inches long, and about a half-inch wide, and you can flip up that little razor blade, and it's serrated. That's exactly the one they show you. You can Google it so that you get the right one. Go ahead and try and cut up a chicken for dinner.

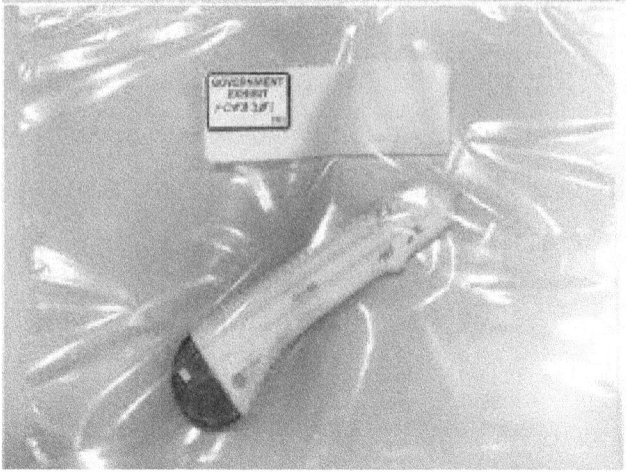

Box cutter found and used at trial

The scenario was that these flight attendants were told that they were the first of however many, maybe they told them four, but I think that they might have actually wanted to have another plane. There's no way that Betty Ong knew unless she was told.

Q. What about any phone calls that came from other flights?

A. Going into the next flight, phone calls were made from two people. The interesting thing about those two was that one was a passenger named Peter Hanson, who was 32-years old at the time, traveling with his wife and small daughter, and he called his dad. He told his dad that, "The airline hostess had been stabbed," three minutes before impact into the South Tower, according to the official story.

We have never been called "Airline Hostess" in the United States of America. Peter Hanson was an American. Airline Hostess is a term used in the Middle East and Asia. El Al, the Israel airline, uses that term. We've been called "flight attendants" since 1968, and before that, we were called a stewardess. In the late sixties, we started hiring men to become flight attendants. So, that was a red flag for me because someone was telling him to say that because he wouldn't have said it in other words. It's not the way we would speak as Americans.

I thought that was odd, and three minutes before impact, he says this to his dad, "I think the terrorists are going to fly us to Chicago and fly us into a building." There's no way that before 911, any one of us would have ever dreamed that as a scenario. Then, he called his dad back again and said a stewardess was stabbed. So, again he used terminology that was very uncommon for a guy his age. The guy was 32.

Peter Burton Hanson was an American software salesman from Groton, Massachusetts. On September 11, 2001, Peter, his wife Sue, and their two-year-old daughter Christine boarded United Airlines Flight 175 from Boston to Los Angeles. Peter made a final call to his parents' moments before the plane crashed into the tower: "It's getting bad, Dad. A stewardess was stabbed. They seem to have knives and mace. They said they have a bomb. Passengers are throwing up and getting sick. The plane is making jerky movements. I don't think the pilot is flying the plane. I think we are going down. I think they intend to go to Chicago or someplace and fly into a building. Don't worry, Dad. If it happens, it'll be very fast. Oh my God, oh my God." The call then ended abruptly.[9]

Then, another guy called, a passenger, and his name was Brian Sweeney. According to the FBI, he was an F14 pilot. He served in the Gulf war of '91, and he trained in Miramar, California, as a top gun sort of pilot. I've actually flown is some top gun pilots, Blue Angels train at Miramar, and these guys are also trained in combat, hand to hand, in case they crash down and become a prisoner of war.

Brian Sweeney was 6'2" and 225 pounds, and his friends said of him that he could kill any human being with his bare hands. On the hijacking day, three minutes before impact, he called his mommy and told his mom that he was on a plane that was hijacked. But he didn't mention the hijackers or anything. He told her that it wasn't looking good, and then she asked him where he was. So, he looked out the window, three minutes before impact in Manhattan, think about this, he said they were over Ohio. I thought that was a weird thing to say because he's a pilot. Even passengers know Manhattan when they see it. New York is like 365 square miles, so you are in New York for a very long time.

If you're close enough to see the ground, which he was at three minutes before impact. They were probably at 6,000 feet at the maximum, and he would know where he was. Then, he said to his mother, and this was eight minutes after the passengers realized that they were hijacked, and started making their phone calls, "We're thinking about taking over the jet from the hijackers, a bunch of us passengers."

Brian Sweeney had been a pilot in the Navy and had worked as an instructor at TOPGUN, Miramar, California. He was medically discharged from the Navy in 1997 after an accident that had left him partially paralyzed. Sweeney is remembered for the emotional voicemail he left for his wife after the plane was hijacked. In the message, he said: "Jules, this is Brian. Listen, I'm on an airplane that's been hijacked. If things don't go well, and it's not looking good, I just want you to know I absolutely love you. I want you to do good. Go have good times. Same to my parents and everybody. And I just totally love you, and I'll see you when you get there. Bye, babe. I hope I call you."[10]

Let me tell you a little secret about flight attendants. You think you're going to take over anything on our airplane, you are wrong. We are highly trained to handle every emergency, including hijackings. We would have told him to sit down and shut up in no uncertain terms. No-one is going to take over the cockpit or the aisle. We've trained for that. That's what we do. That's what we are.

So that scenario, the one from Flight 93, let's roll. Todd Beemer and the heroes from Flight 93 that they made the movies about, how did he know that scenario unless he was either a handler, a planner, or someone had told him of the scenario for later on that day? Let's roll.

Todd Morgan Beamer was an American man aboard United Airlines Flight 93, which was hijacked and crashed as part of the September 11 attacks in 2001. He was one of the passengers who attempted to regain control of the aircraft from the hijackers. During the struggle, the Boeing 757 lost control and crashed into a field in Stonycreek Township near Shanksville, Pennsylvania, killing everyone on-board.[11] Beamer married Brosious on May 14, 1994, in Peekskill, New York, and they moved to Plainsboro, New Jersey, where Beamer began working with Oracle Corporation, selling systems applications and database software as a field marketing representative. Within months, Beamer was promoted to account manager. In 2000, the Beamers moved to Cranbury, New Jersey, with their two sons.[12]

If you think you're going to get up, fill coffee pots with hot water, run up the aisle, and take the cockpit back that way, I'm going to tell you another reason that's not going to happen. Not only would no flight attendant crew members let you do that in a hijacking, but the box also that sits between the Captain and the Copilot is the flight computer, and it's a bit sensitive to the water and liquid.

So, the last thing we would do, when we hand the Captain a glass of juice or water or coffee, it goes over his left shoulder over by the window that wraps around the cockpit, and we say, "Captain Johnson, your coffee is coming in off to the left." Then, he knows to turn around there. Because if he turns around to the right, the computers sitting right under his right shoulder and your hand with that coffee could be hit, or you could hit turbulence. That liquid could jump out, and it doesn't take much to do some computer damage.

The last thing any flight crew will allow is three or four passengers with hot water in coffee pots to run down to the cockpit. By the way, that was the scenario that we are led to believe happened on Flight 93. While the aircraft, according to the FAA and NTSB, was coming out of the sky from 6-to-10,000 feet per minute at an angle of 40 plus degrees and at one-point upside down.

Q. What about Flight 77?

A. Well, then on the third flight, Flight 77, this is really interesting, again we have two people that called out. We had a flight attendant call in, and she called her mom and dad, the last place that you would call. By the way, the Common Strategy from the FAA did not include making phone calls. In real life, if there was a real hijacker on, and he caught you with any kind of a phone to your ear, chances are you'd be dead.

Here's what you'd want to do, word for word from the FAA, you would want to sit down and not draw attention to yourself. So, making phone calls, in themselves, is odd behavior. But she called her mom and dad.

She was a relatively new flight attendant, but still no excuse. We're trained in what to do. She said, "We've been hijacked. Call American Airlines and let them know. We are up in the air." Again, she has to tell them that the hijacking is taking place in the air. If you were going to make a phone call, you would call the right people. A supervisor would probably be the closest person to the right person you would call.

Then, one of my very favorite characters, this is very interesting, Barbara Olson, a CNN commentator, calls into her husband, who was working for George W. Bush Jr. in his Department of Justice. Her husband was Ted Olson, the Solicitor General. She calls his office. Apparently, she doesn't have a direct number for him because she called through his secretary. So, the secretary gets Ted on the phone, and they have three or four little snippets of phone calls.

She's the one that tells the stories about the box cutters that have been used. She also says something else that's really unusual for a flight attendant or airline personal to hear, she says that "The terrorists have heard them all to the very back section of the airplane. They are all sitting back there." She wants Ted to tell her what she should tell the pilots and what they should do. It sounds like the pilots are there, but she never really says that.

Now, Ted, and I don't know a woman that wouldn't kill her husband, and she'd come back from the grave to kill him after this. Ted is so upset that day that he runs right over to the CNN studio to tell his story about how his wife called in and said that they had box cutters, and they were of Middle-eastern descent. This Middle-eastern descent, that terminology was used in a lot of the phone calls.

He is quickly over at the CNN studio, and his story starts to change. It becomes very interesting because, at Zacarias Moussaoui's trial, he is referred to as the twentieth hijacker. Even in the official 911 hearings, Barbara Olson's phone calls are completely not mentioned. Much like building seven that fell down that afternoon was not mentioned.

Now, Ted says that she called collect from her cell phone, and we all know that that's not possible. He said this on CNN. Then, he said that she called from the air-phone. We know that's not possible too since as of January 2001, American Airlines 757s didn't have any air-phones that were functioning.

It's very interesting that Ted Olson had so many stories, and none of them could have been true. I don't have an explanation for that. However, a lot of people who have come forward since the book came out and that have read the book really question and think that Barb Olson might have been part of the planners and may have been one of the hijackers on-board.

I don't know. I never have really looked into her that deeply. But it's very interesting that that whole story was left out of the official story – her phone calls to the Solicitor General for the President of the United States of America, George W. Bush.

Barbara Kay Olson was an American lawyer and conservative television commentator who worked for CNN, Fox News Channel, and several other outlets. She was a passenger on American Airlines Flight 77 en route to a taping of Bill Maher's television show *Politically Incorrect* when it was flown into the Pentagon in the September 11 attacks. Her original plan had been to fly to California on September 10, but she delayed her departure until the next morning so she could wake up with her husband on his birthday, September 11.[13]

Q. So, are you saying that George Bush was involved in this plan?

A. There are some interesting connections to the Bush family. For instance, George Bush Sr. was having a meeting with the senior Bin Laden family member the day before and was also a member of the Carlyle Group.

The Carlyle Group is an American multinational private equity, alternative asset management, and financial services corporation. It specializes in corporate, private equity, real assets, and private credit. In 2015, Carlyle was the world's largest private equity firm by capital raised over the previous five years, according to the PEI 300 index, though by 2020, it had slipped into second place. Founded in 1987 in Washington, D.C., by William E. Conway Jr., Daniel A. D'Aniello, and David Rubenstein, the company today has more than 1,575 employees in 31 offices on six continents. On May 3, 2012, Carlyle completed a $700 million initial public offering and began trading on the NASDAQ stock exchange.[14]

Carlyle has been profiled in two notable documentaries: Michael Moore's *Fahrenheit 9/11* and William Karel's *The World According to Bush*. In *Fahrenheit 9/11*, Moore makes nine allegations concerning the Carlyle Group. Moore focused on Carlyle's connections with George H. W. Bush and his Secretary of State James Baker, both of whom had at times served as advisers to the firm. The movie quotes author Dan Briody, who claimed that the Carlyle Group "gained" from the September 11 attacks because it owned military contractor United Defense.[15]

A Carlyle spokesman noted in 2003 that its 7 percent interest in defense industries was far less than several other private equity firms. In *The World According to Bush*, William Karel interviewed Frank Carlucci to discuss the presence of Shafiq bin Laden, Osama bin Laden's estranged brother, at Carlyle's annual investor conference while the September 11 attacks were occurring.

Q. There were also questions about how George Bush Jr. reacted while he was being told about the 911 attacks while in that classroom with the children.

A. The Secret Service didn't react the way they should in order to protect our President. Whoever our President is, whether we like him or not, their job is to keep our President safe. When you see Andrew Card whispering in his ear, that's after the second plane hit. At that point, you'll remember that most Americans thought we were under attack. That was our Pearl Harbor we were experiencing. I know how I reacted.

We know that he was being told after the second plane hit, and he was sitting there. That was at 9:03 a.m. when that plane hit, and he sat there in that school until after 9:30 a.m. You would think that the Secret Service would have said, "Mr. President, we're out of here." He wouldn't have sat there with those kids. Not only was he in danger, but those kids were too. I found that the Secret Service behavior was most telling. That told me that they knew he wasn't in danger.

By the time you had Andrew Card telling the President, you had CNN on television using the terms "terrorism" and "attack." You can go back and see this, "America under attack" running across the lower banner on CNN. That happened right away.

Andrew Hill Card Jr. is an American politician and academic administrator who was White House Chief of Staff under President George W. Bush from 2001 to 2006, as well as head of Bush's White House Iraq Group. Card served as United States Secretary of Transportation under President George H. W. Bush from 1992 to 1993.[16]

According to Andrew Card's timeline, on September 11, 2001, Bush had just arrived at Emma E. Booker Elementary School in Sarasota,

Fla., and was standing outside of the classroom when at 8:46 a.m. hijackers crashed American Airlines Flight 11 into the North Tower of the World Trade Center in New York City.

The first report Bush and Card received about that crash came just before the president walked into a second-grade class and was initially said to have been a small prop plane. Bush entered the classroom and started reading the story, "The Pet Goat."

As Card waited in another room with White House staff while the president spoke to the class, a U.S. Navy captain told Card that, in fact, it was a commercial jetliner that slammed into one of the Twin Towers. A few minutes later, she exclaimed, "Oh my God, another plane hit the other tower." While standing outside the second-grade classroom where Bush was listening to a reading of the children's book "The Pet Goat," Card was told that a second plane had hit the other World Trade Center Tower. "That's when I knew it couldn't have been an accident. It couldn't have been a coincidence."

Card entered the second-grade classroom at 9:05 a.m. and whispered into the President's ear, "A second plane hit the second tower. America is under attack."

All of the calls from Flight 93, and there were a lot of them, thirty-something. There were 11 calls from 11 people, I think, nine passengers and two flight attendants were taken off the plane and made phone calls. Those phone calls were to only create heroes.

Another thing that was interesting was that another character who was on the phone with his wife the whole time was a Judo champion. He had a Black Belt in Judo, and he was 6 foot and 225 pounds, much like the guy who was the fighter pilot. He sat on the phone and talked to his wife the whole time. Right up until the very minute, we're led to believe that the takeover of the cockpit supposedly took place.

Well, I looked into all of those characters that were supposedly the heroes of Flight 93, let's roll, and all those other guys, well, they were all on the phone in separate rows in coach. Not even close to each other, but on phone calls to other people, and they didn't have any planning time.

Another thing I noticed was that none of the calls from Flight 93 mentioned terrorists or hijackers, but they knew they were going to be killed. You could tell by the things they said, and they were almost all cell phone calls.

That plane supposedly took off at 8:42 a.m., and the phone calls actually started one minute prior to the pilots knowing they were hijacked. The passengers somehow knew prior. At 9:27 a.m., a passenger from California named Tom Burnett called his wife. This is an interesting story because Dana Burnett is a retired flight attendant, and when she looked at her caller ID, it said "Tom cell." So, she knew just like I would that he wasn't on-board for 45 minutes. So, she picked up the phone and said, "Tom, are you okay? What's up?" obviously thinking he didn't get on his flight. So, he tells her again, "We're in the air and on a flight that's been hijacked." Again, he uses the term "We're in the air." This was one minute before the plane was officially hijacked. One minute before, somehow, a passenger knew they were being hijacked. He called her several times, like four times during that day. He also told her that there was a gun on-board, that one of the guys had a gun.

When the FBI gets to her house, they argue that point with her. I think the reason they argue that point with her is they didn't want the security company to be tagged. Guess who ran security at Boston, Washington, Dulles, and Newark for those two airlines? It was a company called ITS, and they were an Israeli security company, not a U.S. Corporation, an Israeli security company, coincidently.

So, what I'm finding as I'm looking through this is that this weird connection, we've got an Israeli-trained assassin on Flight 93, and we have a Jewish Judo champion on Flight 11. On Flight 93, we have a Jewish Judo champion that chooses to do nothing but sit and talk on the phone with his wife.

Then, I start to look at some of the other passengers on-board. I've also been contacted by people from American Airlines that guarantee there were no Arab passengers on the real passenger manifest.

Here's something else that most people don't know because I didn't, and I paid close attention. The FBI originally claimed they had the passenger manifest right away from the four flights. And of the 19 Arab hijackers, there were four different names originally that you don't even know they were switched out. Those four people, three of them showed up alive.

So, about 72 hours into the event, they changed those four names but not the other guys who were the Saudi Air and Air Tunisia pilots, or those who were working outside of Rhihad in an energy business that has never seen America and didn't even know what Pennsylvania was. They are still alive.

So, they had these four people that the FBI claimed were actually on the passenger list. They put it out there. It was on CNN. One of these characters is an FAA employee in aviation safety based in Florida. His brother had been killed one year earlier, on September 11, 2000. So, he called in and said, "I'm not a hijacker. They are telling everybody on TV that me and my brother. We are not on the passenger list. How can we be on the passenger manifest? I was at work." The other two gentlemen showed up alive and well.

But the FBI told America that these four guys were on the passenger manifest list, and they were lying to you. Until those people showed up, three of them alive and one dead, they didn't change their story. The FBI is the biggest part of the cover-up. I found in an FBI document that potentially one, maybe two, women were involved. When I was in final edits, I found the women who were involved. I felt a spiritual presence in my room when I found that. The FBI was covering up women involved, perpetrators, planners, handlers, and you don't even know they exist. I'm the only 911 truth investigator that has found them. It's in an FBI document, and I just got it off the internet.

Q. What was the specific reason for the FBI not coming forward about two women being involved?

A. Because they wanted you to think they were all Arabs. These two women were not Arab.

Q. What do you think happened with the planes?

A. When I went through all of those phone calls, I realized that they were all there just to grab our emotions and get us hooked into this. These were people who were calling to say goodbye, and I love you. You can look this up, a flight attendant from Flight 93, that's the one that supposedly crashed into Shanksville, CeeCee Lyles, called her husband and kids and left a recording at 9:47 a.m., about 15 minutes before the plane crashed. At the end of her call, you can hear her hand the phone to somebody else. Then, you can hear a woman's voice tell CeeCee Lyles, "You did great." Go ahead and right click and save the recording if you can because the government will be removing this. (It still up at the writing of this book in February of 2021)

But I found it right there online in front of our faces. Just like the Illuminati love to do. Just like in March of 2001, they put this TV show on called, *The Lone Gunman*. It basically was a scenario when these planes were taken over and being flown into the World Trade Center.

Q. So what are you saying really happened then?

A. I started thinking that this was a very poorly written script. Someone who doesn't know that cell phones don't work at altitude, and they don't know what a flight attendant would allow to happen in an aisle during a hijacking. They don't know the code words or protocol. That's why the story came out the way that it did.

I remember in the '90s that there was a company called SPC Corporation that sold to Boeing a device that fits right into the Boeing onboard flight computer called the "Flight Termination System." This system is a plugin device to an on-board flight computer, sold to some flight carriers in the event of a hijacking. If a hijacker took control of the cockpit, we could land the airplane remotely.

Q. Why didn't they land those planes remotely then?

A. It's because those systems were already in use by the perpetrators, planners, and handlers, and not 19 Arabs. When the Flight Termination System takes over, it uses the same frequency as the flight transponder. It also makes it so the pilots can no longer speak to anyone on the ground, or other airplanes, or the flight attendants in the back.

Remember Betty Ong said that the pilots weren't answering their phones, and that told me the Flight Termination System had landed the aircraft. They were on the ground, no longer pressurized 20 minutes after they left Boston.

So, all of the phone calls from all four aircraft had to have been made from the ground because it's impossible to call from a cell phone. It would have been about 45 minutes into the flight, so they would have been 32- and 39,000-feet elevation.

Q. Where did they take the planes to?

A. Because all of these aircraft were loaded up with fuel, they would have had to have at least a 10,000-foot runway that was not a commercial airport. I found the location where all four were brought. The phone calls were then made. I believe it was at a C5 transportation base located in Massachusetts. A C5 transport is larger than a 747. After the book was published, I heard from someone who was in the reserves, and she told me the name of the base. She told me that she was stationed there and that the base was evacuated.

When she got called up for active duty the day of 911, they were locked out of that base and put up in hotels for two to three days.

What we think happened was that the crews were told this was part of a drill, and ongoing that day were over a dozen military war games across our country. There was a lot of confusion that day, and even when air traffic control called NORAD, they were told there was a hijacking on Flight 11. They thought it was part of a drill. Some of the drills were actually airplanes being hijacked and flown into buildings.

Because of those war games that Dick Cheney rescheduled to happen on September 11, a lot of them were supposed to happen in October. A lot of our jets we would have thought would scramble to save the aircraft were on the other side of the country or over the Atlantic Ocean.

So, they probably told the pilots that they were part of these drills. When they took the two people off each of the aircraft to make phone calls, a canister of some sort of lethal gas was put in the aircraft, and the door was shut. Before the flight crews could figure out that it wasn't a drill and it wasn't fake, they had enough gas in them to make them unable to save the passengers or themselves. Those first two planes came in about 15 minutes apart, so they had quite a few people to get rid of.

Q. What was the reason behind taking these planes?

A. There was a need for what they called "The New Pearl Harbor" in order to manipulate and get the American public to rally behind seven planned wars in the Middle East. Currently, there's a lot of misinformation coming from the media, which is all controlled by the CIA. They manipulate us as groups to hate each other and to hate others.

Right after 911, we started losing rights. By the way, the Patriot Act was written before 911, and we were ready to go with that. We now have the NDAA where they can drone strike us on our own property if they feel we're a threat to them.

Listen to the full interview with Rebekah Roth on my website:

houseofmysteryradio/episodes/methodical-illusion-rebekah-roth

Interview Afterthoughts

How can anybody write a non-fiction true event book and add several fictional characters to it? Well, that's easy, Rebekah Roth did it in her book, and I would guess that it's because it was a great way for you to get your conspiracy theory mixed into reality without having to worry about getting sued for it.

This seems to be the popular thing to do these days, write books that are supposed to be non-fiction, research presenting the facts about true events that have happened. Only many of these books are written with a fiction element to them, where the author claims it's to fill in the holes and let the reader decide what the truth is. But the issue then becomes the problem of the reader having to decide which parts of the book are true and really happened and which parts are fiction and created.

Roth is a great spokesperson to present such a book. She is a good Christian woman who believes in right and wrong. She has always worked a regular job, like her readers, and tried to live a normal life. So, the interview started out quite nicely, and she sounded very reasonable.

But it wasn't too long before she started getting into the idea that the planes never crashed into the towers or the Pentagon and that it wasn't a real event. She believes the planes were actually taken and forced to land, where they forced people to make rehearsed phone calls to their loved ones.

It got even crazier when she asked me if I had known that there was a Jew on each of the planes. My first thought was, why would that matter. After all, there would have to be a good chance of a few Jewish people being on each

254 CONSPIRACY THEORY CULTURE

plane when there was a couple of hundred passengers.

She continued on to tell me that they were trained by the Mossad, which is part of the Israeli Intelligence Community. You see, she believes they were placed on-board to do the hijackings of the planes and to make it look like the real hijackers were Arab. This way, the United States and most of the world would end up hating and starting a war against the Arabs.

Roth even went as far as to tell callers of the show that there never were planes that flew into the towers, even though the callers were there in New York and saw it with their own eyes. So, even when a witness to the planes crashing into the towers confronted Roth on her theories, she told them that, "They only thought they saw it."

If anything, it sounded like a really bad B-movie that you'd see late at night where even the advertisements had more truth. I think the only thing that she brought up that deserved some research was whether someone could call from a jet plane while flying to someone on the ground. Which a lot of people started researching, and yes, of course, they could, as long as they were within a certain distance to the ground, which they were.

Bottom line: The book isn't even a good crime fiction story.

---

1. Thu Jan 17 - Rebekah Roth - A Flight Attendant's 9/11 ....
   https://midnightinthedesert.com/rebekah-roth/
2. Al-Qaeda - Wikipedia. https://en.wikipedia.org/wiki/Al-Qaida_Al-Jihad
3. American Airlines Flight 11 - Simple English Wikipedia .... https://simple.m.wikipedia.org/wiki/American_Airlines_Flight_11
4. Boeing 767-300ER | Five Airways. https://fiveairways.com/product/boeing-767-300er/
5. Betty Ong - Wikipedia. https://en.wikipedia.org/wiki/Betty_Ong
6. Inside The Terrifying Final Minutes of Brave 9/11 Victims https://www.transportationnation.com/inside-the-terrifying-final-minutes-of-brave-9-11-victims/
7. Sayeret Matkal - Wikipedia. https://en.wikipedia.org/wiki/Sayeret_Matkal
8. Daniel Lewin - Wikipedia. https://en.wikipedia.org/wiki/Daniel_Lewin
9. Peter Hanson | Gone Too Soon Wiki | Fandom. https://gonetoosoon.fandom.com/wiki/Peter_Hanson
10. Who Was Brian Sweeney? 9/11 Victim Who Left Heartfelt https://www.newsweek.com/brian-sweeney-911-victim-1530935
11. Todd Beamer - Wikipedia. https://en.wikipedia.org/wiki/Todd_Beamer
12. Todd Beamer - Alchetron, The Free Social Encyclopedia. https://alchetron.com/Todd-Beamer

13. Tyrannic   Officers: September   2016.   https://
    tyrannicofficers.blogspot.com/2016/09/
14. The Carlyle Group - Infogalactic: the planetary knowledge
    core. https://infogalactic.com/info/The_Carlyle_Group
15. The Carlyle Group - Wikipedia. https://en.wikipedia.org/
    wiki/The_Carlyle_Group
16. Andrew   Card   -   Wikipedia.   https://en.wikipedia.org/
    wiki/Andrew_Card

FDR Let Pearl Harbor Happen

The Conspiracy Theory

During that last interview with the 911 truther Rebekah Roth, she mentioned something about the Pearl Harbor attack being planned by the U.S. government, or being what she called a "False Flag." Could that be true that our government either set up the bombing, staged it, or perhaps just let it happen?

Well, I had to follow this up, and I got Robert Stinnett to agree to a phone interview. It's really hard to find people that were alive during the bombing at Pearl Harbor. If you do find someone, they are elderly and not up to doing an interview.

We did this interview in 2014 when Stinnett was 90-years old, and I was broadcasting over the KFNX 1150 A.M. station in Phoenix.

Interview with Robert B. Stinnett

Robert B. Stinnett was an American sailor, photographer, and author. He earned ten battle stars and a Presidential Unit Citation. He was the author of *Day of Deceit*, regarding alleged U.S. government advance knowledge of the Japanese attack on Pearl Harbor, plunging the United States into World War II.

Stinnett participated in World War II from 1942 to 1946 as a naval photographer in the Pacific theater, serving in the same aerial photo group as George H. W. Bush. After the war, he worked as a journalist and photographer for the *Oakland Tribune*. He resigned from the *Tribune* in 1986 to research and write.

Stinnett was a research fellow at the Independent Institute in Oakland, California. He died on November 6, 2018, aged 94.[1]

Q. Robert, tell the listeners a little bit about yourself?

A. I joined the Navy on December 1, 1942, and was assigned to the USS San Jacinto, which was a light aircraft carrier of the Pacific fleet. One of our officers was Ensign George Bush. He was the photographic officer of the torpedo squadron. As you could guess, it was George H. W. Bush who became President of the United States. So, we both learned Aerial photography and used it against the Japanese navy in World War II.

USS San Jacinto of the United States Navy was an Independence-class light aircraft carrier that served during World War II. She was named for the Battle of San Jacinto during the Texas Revolution. Former U.S. President George H.W. Bush served aboard the ship during World War II. San Jacinto joined in the first carrier strikes against the home islands of Japan. During the raids on 16 and 17 February 1945, carrier-based aircraft shot down many enemy planes during fierce dogfights over airfields in the Tokyo area. These operations were designed to cover the imminent invasion of Iwo Jima. Next came air support for the landing Marines, followed by further strikes against Tokyo and Okinawa before San Jacinto returned to Ulithi.

On 7 April, San Jacinto's bombers torpedoed the Japanese destroyers Hamakaze and Asashimo, part of a naval suicide attack in which super battleship Yamato was also sunk. San Jacinto then returned to the dangerous job of defending against the suicide plane attacks, striking at the kamikaze airfields on Kyūshū, and providing close air support for ground forces fighting on Okinawa.

San Jacinto was decommissioned on March 1, 1947, and joined the Pacific Reserve Fleet berthed at San Diego. She was reclassified as an auxiliary aircraft transport (AVT-5) on May 15, 1959, and struck from the Navy list on June 1, 1970; her hull was sold for scrapping in December 1971.[2]

Q. Did you get to know George Bush very well?

A. Yes. He was a very dedicated pilot, but he was also in charge of Aerial Photography. So, he would come back to the photo lab on the San Jacinto, and we would discuss the photos for each day and how the photography would be accomplished. He would always joke with us, and there was never any photographer put-downs to us from him.

Q. Did you ever think that he would become President?

A. I had no idea. But I liked him so much I took a lot of photographs of him. A lot of the photographs I took of him were used later on in his campaigns.

Aerial Photography is a transformational growth in air reconnaissance that occurred in the years 1939–45, especially in Britain and then in the United States. It was an expansion determined mostly by trial and error, represented mostly by new tactics, new procedures, and new technology, though rarely by specialized aircraft types. The mission type branched out into many sub-types,

262 CONSPIRACY THEORY CULTURE

including new electronic forms of reconnaissance. In sharp contrast with the case during the pre-war years, by 1945, air reconnaissance was widely recognized as a vital, indispensable component of airpower.[3]

Q. Let's talk about your book *Day of Deceit* and how you came to write it.

A. I was very interested in the attack at Pearl Harbor that was used by President Roosevelt as a means to get us into the war in 1941. So, I was reading all sorts of military books put out by others from the East Coast university Ivy-leaguers. In 1982, I read a book by Gordon Prange called *At Dawn we Slept*.

In the book, he talked about an intercept station or a monitoring station that was listening to the Japanese Imperial Navy radio broadcast. Well, it was the first I had heard of that. It was top secret, and we were not discussing it aboard the San Jacinto. So, I wanted to find out more about the station because if we were listening to the Japanese orders to their fleet, then Pearl Harbor could not have been a secret attack.

I worked at the time at the *Oakland Tribune*, and I thought that this monitoring station, if it existed, would be a good December 7, 1982 story for Pearl Harbor. I talked to my editor about it, and he told me to go over to Hawaii and see if that's true.

So, I filed a Freedom of Information with the Navy about the monitoring station, and they granted it to me, believe it or not. So, I went over there too and met some of the radio operators who were guides at the facility at Pearl Harbor around the USS Arizona.

That's where I met the cryptographers who were listening to the messages, and they told me where I would find more information. That sent me to the National Archives that I'm still using in my 22 or 23 year.

Q. At the time, you were a sailor. What were your feelings toward FDR? Did you think that he was a good President?

A. Oh, yes. I supported him. In fact, he was the first President I ever voted for. That was in 1944. But prior to that, I was a great admirer of him. He was trying to establish aircraft carriers to fight Germany. I was quite aware of the isolation movement in this country that did not want to get involved in Europe's war. I was sort of a news junkie teenager at the time, and I would listen to Edward R. Murrow and the networks, which were reporting what was going on in Germany.

During the 1930s, the combination of the Great Depression and the memory of tragic losses in World War I contributed to pushing American public opinion and policy toward isolationism. Isolationists advocated non-involvement in European and Asian conflicts and non-entanglement in international politics.[4]

On September 1, 1939, Germany invaded Poland; Britain and France subsequently declared war on Germany, marking the start of World War II. In an address to the American people two days later, President Roosevelt assured the nation that he would do all he could to keep them out of the war. However, his words showed his true goals, "When peace has been broken anywhere, the peace of all countries everywhere is in danger," Roosevelt said. Even though he was intent on neutrality as the official policy of the United States, he still echoed the dangers of staying out of this war. He also cautioned the American people to not let their wish to avoid war at all costs supersede the security of the nation.

The war in Europe split the American people into two camps: non-interventionists and interventionists. The two sides argued over America's involvement in this World War II. The basic principle of the interventionist argument was fear of German invasion.[5]

Q. Did people not realize what was going on in Europe?

A. Well, of course, it was all secret what was going on in Europe. Also, how to do away with the isolation movement in this country and get the United States to fight Germany again in World War II was a problem. Because in World War I, we made a lot of loans to European countries. We sent our troops over there, and they were gassed by the Germans in the battlefields of Europe. Americans wanted nothing to do with another world war.

That was the situation the President faced in the late 1930s early 1940s. So, he was trying to use deceit to get us into the war by getting Japan to attack us. Japan was using deceit to hide all of this. So, it was deceit versus deceit. The U.S. Navy found out all about this because we were monitoring the Japanese Naval radio network. We had monitoring stations in San Diego, Seattle, Dutch Harbor, and down on the China coast, and into the Philippines. We had Japan wired for sound, but they also had us wired because they had a spy hidden in the Japanese Counsel in Hawaii who arrived in March 1941. He began spying on the Pacific Fleet.

Then in the late summer of '41, he started preparing bomb plots of the Pearl Harbor anchorage where these warships were anchored. He sent them back on RCA radio communications in Honolulu, and the FBI was alerted to it. But this was all kept secret, part of the deceit.

So, Japan was using deceit to learn about the Pacific Fleet, and we're trying to get them to attack us. That's what happened about 14 months before Pearl Harbor, when President Roosevelt summoned the Commander of the Fleet to the White House, into the Oval Office, and told him about this plan.

The Admiral blew up at the President, and there was a heated conversation. But you don't talk to the President like Richardson did. In October 1940, he was in charge of the U.S. Fleet until Admiral Richardson opposed President Roosevelt when he proposed getting Japan to attack us at Pearl Harbor and trigger a treaty with Germany, Italy, and Japan that would state they would come to one another's aid.

This is a backdoor approach to get us into the war with Germany. They're the ones that Roosevelt feared, not really Japan. So, he adopted a plan by the Navy to get Japan to come in and go to war against the United States.

James Otto Richardson was an admiral in the United States Navy who served from 1902 to 1947. As Commander in Chief of the United States Fleet, he protested the redeployment of the Pacific portion of the fleet forward to Pearl Harbor since he believed that a forward defense was neither practical nor useful and that the Pacific Fleet would be the logical first target in the event of war with Japan since it was vulnerable to air and torpedo attacks. He was relieved of command in February 1941. His concerns proved justified during the Japanese attack on Pearl Harbor only ten months later.[6]

Q. What do you think the general feeling was towards Japan, before the Pearl Harbor attack, within the United States?

A. In my high school, we had Japanese students in the class, and we were all very friendly and loved all the students. But

Roosevelt saw this opportunity when Japan signed the Tripartite Pact with Germany and Italy in September 1940. The Tripartite Pact was that those were the Axis Nations, and if one was attacked by another nation that was not in the war at the time, meaning the United States, then the other nations would come to their aid. So, Roosevelt adopted a Navy plan seizing on this deal that they would come to one another's aid.

The Tripartite Pact, also known as the Berlin Pact, was an agreement between Germany, Italy, and Japan signed in Berlin on September 27, 1940, by, respectively, Joachim von Ribbentrop, Galeazzo Ciano, and Saburō Kurusu. It was a defensive military alliance that was eventually joined by Hungary (20 November 1940), Romania (23 November 1940), Bulgaria (1 March 1941), and Yugoslavia (25 March 1941), as well as by the German client state of Slovakia (24 November 1940).

- ARTICLE 1. Japan recognizes and respects

the leadership of Germany and Italy in the establishment of a new order in Europe.

- ARTICLE 2. Germany and Italy recognize and respect the leadership of Japan in the establishment of a new order in Greater East Asia.
- ARTICLE 3. Japan, Germany, and Italy agree to cooperate in their efforts on aforesaid lines. They further undertake to assist one another with all political, economic, and military means if one of the Contracting Powers is attacked by a Power at present not involved in the European War or in the Japanese-Chinese conflict.
- ARTICLE 4. With a view to implementing the present pact, joint technical commissions, to be appointed by the respective Governments of Japan, Germany, and Italy, will meet without delay.
- ARTICLE 5. Japan, Germany, and Italy affirm that the above agreement affects in no way the political status existing at present between each of the three Contracting Powers and Soviet Russia.

- ARTICLE 6. The present pact shall become valid immediately upon signature and shall remain in force ten years from the date on which it becomes effective. In due time, before the expiration of said term, the High Contracting Parties shall, at the request of any one of them, enter into negotiations for its renewal.[7]

Q. So, how exactly did Roosevelt provoke Japan into attack the U.S.?

A. There were eight provocations to provoke Japan into attacking us at Pearl Harbor, and he adopted all eight of them starting in October 1940. We were following from our monitoring stations. One of those stations was in Seattle, on Bainbridge Island, called "Station Sugar." In Sugar, the S was for Seattle.

Q. What was Roosevelt's plan then?

A. Well, he adopted a navy plan from a Lieutenant Commander who was head of the Far East section of the United States

Navy. He was stationed in Washington D.C. He came up with this war plan to provoke Japan into attacking us at Pearl Harbor. His name was Arthur McCollum. He was a son of Baptist Ministry parents living in Japan, who were teaching Baptist Christian theories to the Japanese. He was also born in Japan and knew the Japanese language very well.

He came up with the plan to keep the U.S. Fleet at Pearl Harbor in order to provoke Japan. So, Roosevelt moved the fleet there in the spring of 1941, with only Admiral Richardson objecting. That was one of the provocations.

Another one was to send American Task Force into Japanese territorial waters to upset their task force. They were also supplying China who was in a war with Japan. They also had an oil and steel embargo against Japan.

McCollum, a key figure to the Office of Naval Intelligence, was the chief commander of the Far

East section of ONI. He served on the staff of the Commander of the U.S Pacific Fleet as the intelligence officer from 1936 to 1938 and served several roles in intelligence from 1942 to 1945.[8]

Q. So, if Roosevelt did this plan, do you think he thought it would be as devastating as it was with so many casualties?

A. The public was led by Charles Lindbergh and the America-First Committee, Henry Ford, and the Hearst newspapers. These groups wanted nothing to do with the war in Europe. They did not want to send their children to another war and go through what they did from 1914 to 1918. According to the Gallup poll at the time, 80 percent of Americans wanted nothing to do with the war.

Commander McCollum knew that the Americans would be so outraged by an attack on Pearl Harbor that they would join in the movement to defeat Germany. That's what it was about. He knew that it would unify the people.

Q. What are your thoughts on the Japanese internment camps?

A. There was only one Japanese spy, and his name was Yoshikawa. He was the one sending the messages. But because of people's knowledge of this, Roosevelt simply ordered 120,000 Americans with Japanese ancestry into concentration camps in February 1942. In the meantime, the Japanese consulate in Honolulu was taken into protective custody and sent to a dude ranch in Arizona, in luxury conditions, to hide the consulate and the spy from American newspapermen.

Takeo Yoshikawa was a Japanese spy in Hawaii before the attack on Pearl Harbor on December 7, 1941, and because of his expertise on the U.S. Navy, Yoshikawa was sent to Hawaii posing as a vice-consul named Tadashi Morimura, arriving on March 27, 1941, with Nagao Kita, the new Japanese Consul-General.

He gathered information by taking the Navy's own harbor tugboat and listening to local gossip.

According to Yoshikawa, although some 160,000 persons of Japanese ancestry lived in Hawaii at that time, he never tried to make use of this resource in his espionage activities.

Although he had no knowledge of a planned attack on Naval Station Pearl Harbor, Yoshikawa assumed that the intelligence would help prepare for such an eventuality and worked tirelessly to that end. His reports were transmitted by the Japanese consulate in PURPLE code to the Foreign Ministry, which passed them on to the Navy. Although the code had been broken by Allied codebreakers and messages to and from Tokyo were intercepted and decrypted, communications between Tokyo and the consulate were considered a low priority because they contained so many messages that were entirely commercial in nature.

However, one such message addressed to Kita but actually meant for Yoshikawa and sent on September 24, 1941, should have received more attention. It divided Pearl Harbor into five distinct zones and requested that the location and number of warships be indicated on a plot of the harbor. However, due to delays caused by staff shortages and other priorities, the message was not decrypted and distributed until mid-October and then dismissed as being of little consequence. However, it was the reports that he sent twice a week based on this request that enabled Admiral Isoroku Yamamoto to finalize his plan for the attack.[9]

So, they were visiting a dude ranch while 100,000 Japanese-Americans lost the homes and property and were sent to concentration camps in California, Arizona, and other parts of the west. All of a sudden, all of the Japanese disappeared, and we were never told where they all went.

Japanese Internment Camps – The surprise attack on Pearl Harbor on December 7, 1941, led military and political leaders to suspect that Imperial Japan was preparing a full-scale invasion of Hawaii and the West Coast of the United States. Due to Japan's rapid military conquest of a large portion of Asia and the Pacific, including a small portion of the U.S. West Coast between

1937 and 1942, some Americans feared that its military forces were unstoppable.

American public opinion initially stood by the large population of Japanese-Americans living on the West Coast, with the *Los Angeles Times* characterizing them as "good Americans, born and educated as such." Many Americans believed that their loyalty to the United States was unquestionable. However, six weeks after the attack, public opinion along the Pacific began to turn against Japanese-Americans living on the West Coast, as the press and other Americans became nervous about the potential for fifth column activity.

Though the administration, including President Franklin D. Roosevelt and FBI Director J. Edgar Hoover, dismissed all rumors of Japanese-American espionage on behalf of the Japanese war effort, pressure mounted upon the administration as the tide of public opinion turned against Japanese-Americans. More than 112,000 Japanese-Americans living on the West Coast were forced into interior camps. However, in Hawaii, which was under martial law, 150,000-plus Japanese-Americans composed over one-third of the population, only 1,200 to 1,800 were also interned. Sixty-two percent of the internees were United States citizens.[10]

Q. Now that you know what FDR did, do you think it was the right thing for him to do?

A. It was his only option if Germany would have invaded England and got their bases there. Then, in Canada, we'd be toast. Our Ocean Navy did not come into existence until November 1943. Germany and Japan both had substantial Navies with aircraft carriers. Germany also had a huge submarine force. It would have really hurt us badly if we had not got into the war.

Listen to the full interview with Robert B. Stinnett on my website:

https://shows.acast.com/
houseofmysteryradio/
episodes/bob-stinnett-day-of-
deceit

Interview Afterthoughts

On December 7, 1941, Japanese military forces attacked the United States naval fleet anchored at Pearl Harbor on the Hawaiian island of Oahu. The surprise attack was devastating to the U.S. Navy. Nearly every American plane on Oahu was destroyed, including three cruisers, three destroyers, and eight battleships were severely damaged, with two battleships, the Oklahoma and Arizona, destroyed and over 2,300 U.S. servicemen lost their lives.[11]

In the weeks and months that followed, fears ran deep among shocked Americans that Japan had the ability to launch an invasion on the West Coast of the United States. At the very least, it was feared that the Japanese Navy, facing only the remnants of a tattered American fleet, could effectively control the Pacific Ocean, cutting the United States off from vital resources and shipping lanes.

The official investigations into the Japanese attack started in the 1940s, and even now, each time new documents become declassified, a headline pops up asking whether Roosevelt allowed it. Roosevelt was totally caught off guard by it, and the record is clear. There was no evidence of the Japanese moving toward Pearl Harbor that was picked up in Washington. That's not to say that the White House might not have expected some kind of attack from Japan.

After speaking with Bob Stinnett, I knew he was a true American patriot and that his intentions were good. I think his research was done well. He sought out primary sources and took the time to meet with them and ask questions. I have no doubt that what he says is true.

The problem lies with whether FDR was notified about any of these messages that had been decrypted about the Pearl Harbor bombing and when exactly were these coded messages broken. Conspiracy theories, half-truths, and full-on lies are getting new attention as they appear alongside real news and information on social media.[12]

The first thing that Stinnett brought up in our conversation was about Commander McCollum being the one that was given the task of getting Japan to attack America. This is solely based on a Navy Intelligence memo that was declassified in 1994. The memo was sent from McCollum to Navy Captain Walter S. Anderson on November 7, 1940. That memo contained the line, *"If by these means Japan could be led to commit an overt act of war, so much the better."* This line in itself doesn't mean that he wanted Japan to attack us in the devastating way in which the Pearl Harbor attack was, or even that he was doing something on purpose to make them attack America. Evidence the memo or derivative works actually reached President Roosevelt, senior administration officials, or the highest levels of U.S. Navy command, is circumstantial, at best.[13]

The other major claim by Stinnett, as well as most conspiracy theorists that are around, is that not only had the Americans broke the Japanese codes, but they had notified Roosevelt of what the messages said about attacking Pearl Harbor. The highest security diplomatic code, called "Purple" by the Americans, which was used by the Foreign Office and only for diplomatic and not for military messages, was broken by Army cryptographers in 1940. The 14-part message using this code, sent from Japan to its Embassy in Washington, was decoded in Washington on the 6th and 7th of December. The message, which made plain the Japanese intention to break off diplomatic relations with the United States, was to be delivered by the Japanese Ambassador at 1 p.m. Washington time.

A warning message was sent to American bases in the area, including Hawaii. Due to atmospheric transmission conditions, the message was sent out via Western Union over its undersea cable rather than over the military radio channels. The message was not received until the attack was already underway.

The claim that no pre-attack message expressly mentioned Pearl Harbor is perhaps true. The claim that no "Purple" messages pointed to Pearl Harbor may also be true, as the Foreign Office was not well thought of by the military and, during this period, was routinely excluded from sensitive or secret material, including war planning. It is also possible any such intercepts were not translated until after the attack, or indeed after the war ended. The real progress on the Purple code wasn't achieved until late 1942.

Another point I want to bring up is the fact that when I asked Stinnett at least four or five times if he believed Roosevelt not only knew about this plan but was part of it, he wouldn't give a clear answer and diverted the question. I believe it's because, in his heart, he didn't truly believe that Roosevelt was involved.

It might be more about the fact that America was caught unprepared, and for a lot of people, instead of just accepting it, they have to believe that there was a larger group of conspirators working the plan behind everyone's back. There's no way that we could lose due to our own negligence.

---

1. Robert Stinnett - Wikipedia. https://en.wikipedia.org/wiki/Robert_Stinnett
2. USS San Jacinto (CVL-30) - Wikipedia. https://en.wikipedia.org/wiki/USS_San_Jacinto_(CVL-30)

3. Aerial reconnaissance in World War II - Wikipedia. https://en.wikipedia.org/ wiki/Aerial_reconnaissance_in_World_War_II

4. American Isolationism in the 1930s. https://2001-2009. state.gov/r/pa/ho/time/wwii/102129.htm

5. The History of American Foreign Policy | Boundless .... https://courses.lumenlearning.com/boundless-politicalscience/chapter/the-history-of-american-foreign-policy/

6. James O. Richardson - Wikipedia. https://en.wikipedia. org/wiki/James_O._Richardson

7. Tripartite Pact - Wikipedia. https://en.wikipedia.org/ wiki/Axis_Pact

8. Arthur H. McCollum - Wikipedia. https://en.wikipedia. org/wiki/Arthur_H._McCollum

9. Takeo Yoshikawa - Wikipedia. https://en.wikipedia.org/ wiki/Takeo_Yoshikawa

10. Internment of Japanese Americans - Wikipedia. https:// en.wikipedia.org/wiki/Japanese-American_internment_camps

11. World War II, United States Breaking of Japanese Naval .... https://www.encyclopedia.com/politics/encyclopedias-almanacs-transcripts-and-maps/world-war-ii-united-states-breaking-japanese-naval-codes

12. A Fake Story That Lives On: No, FDR Did Not Know The https://www.npr.org/2016/12/06/504449867/no-fdr-did-not-know-the-japanese-were-going-to-bomb-pearl-harbor

13. Pearl Harbor advance-knowledge conspiracy theory - Wikipedia. https://en.wikipedia.org/wiki/Pearl_Harbor_advance-knowledge_conspiracy_theory

Marilyn Monroe was Murdered

❦

The Conspiracy Theory

American filmmaker and producer Paul Davids' films are known for controversy. Beginning with *Roswell*, a 1994 nominee for Golden Globe as Best TV Motion Picture, which he executive produced and co-wrote as a Showtime original movie. It dealt with issues of extraterrestrial life and the purported "truth embargo" on the subject of ET contact.

Davids' many books and films enjoyed a 2018 resurgence. His film, *The Sci-Fi Boys* starring Peter Jackson, was on display through September 2018 at the Pasadena History Museum in their exhibit called "Dreaming the Universe." *Jesus in India* had an Italian premiere at the Odeon Theater in Florence, Italy, in May that year. His film *The Life After Death Project* was featured in June at the Fortfest in Baltimore, a Fortean conference. Paul also presented on the follow-up book to that film, *An Atheist in Heaven: The Ultimate Evidence for Life After Death*.

His film, *Marilyn Monroe Declassified*, "balances the image of the blonde bombshell icon we thought we knew with information about her revealed in newly declassified FBI and CIA files. Here is the proof that her troubles were not all the product of her upbringing in an orphanage, abuse of prescription drugs, and failed marriages. Beginning with her wedding to Communist-leaning playwright Arthur Miller, for whom she converted to Judaism, she was tailed, targeted, and tormented by the FBI, CIA, and Mafia. Ultimately, through affairs with powerful men, she was unwittingly caught in the middle of a vendetta of lethal forces. Dead at age 36, just months after singing "Happy Birthday, Mr. President" at JFK's extravagant party, she was officially listed as a "probable suicide." The film makes a powerful case for the idea that the official conclusion was wrong. The film featured an interview with Greg Schreiner and Pierre Vudrag, Paul Davids on *Bigger Questions*."[1]

Interview with Paul Davids

Q. How did you get into Marilyn Monroe and her death enough to make a film about it?

A. Well, I had recently finished the *Life After Death Project* film, and it was on Sci-Fi. It was an examination of a particularly fascinating case about life after death. I was always aware that there was quite a controversy about Marilyn Monroe's death, which had been ruled at the time, in 1962, a probable suicide. Yet the controversy and objection to that started almost immediately. So, it has always been in the back of my mind, and I thought that maybe the circumstances of her death were unresolved and covered up.

Since I was curious about the realm of spirit communication from the afterlife and had had an experience with a psychic detective, Dorothy Allison, when I was the producer of F. Lee Bailey's *The Lie Detector Show*, I had a very open mind to the possibility. Someone suggested that Marilyn's spirit was very disquieted because people still think she committed suicide, and she didn't.

So, that was one thing. The other thing was that I happened to be invited to film original color separation negatives. These are very, very large negatives that are in bullet-proof plastic. There were over 20 of them of Marilyn's Golden Dreams Calendar photos, which was the famous nude that was controversial from very early on in her career. When I filmed those, there were other people present that talked about the history of Marilyn's life. I thought that maybe there's something real here. This could become an original feature documentary.

Q. How did you deal with all of the rumors and conspiracies about Marilyn? Was it easy to separate the real from the fake?

A. There was a fake news story within the last year declaring a CIA agent who had confessed on his death bed to having murdered Marilyn. It had clues that it was made up because it talked about her affair with Fidel Castro, which is completely absurd. But people don't know right away that when these fake stories come out, they are being used. And that they need to be completely dismissed. That was pretty much an easy one because it came from a known site for those kinds of things. I'm very cautious about what to accept.

In *Marilyn Declassified*, I've got really firm evidence from the real people, the witnesses, their testimonies, and statements that go back to the year of her death. I'm dealing with the people who were actually involved and what they had to say, and how it changed over the years. There were secrets kept that people began to recant after about 20 years, and they changed what they said. Their changes had become more consistent with other things that we know that made us feel that there was a massive cover-up.

There were two police chiefs of Los Angeles, Daryl Gates and Tom Reddin, who both indicated a cover-up years after. Well, Daryl Gates now indicates that Bobby Kennedy had been in town on the day of her death. That's something Bobby Kennedy had always denied. So, you have to ask why. Why was his presence in Los Angeles being covered up at that time? Tom Reddin, the other police chief, said that Marilyn's death was handled as a top-secret intelligence operation, which meant that there was disinformation issued and that facts were withheld. So, you want to get to the source, the original people. Then, find out what's new and what do I add to this mystery that's been going on all these years.

Thomas Reddin was a Los Angeles Police Department chief from 1967 to 1969. He left on

May 6, 1969, to become a news commentator. He also owned a private security company in Los Angeles called the Tom Reddin Security. Reddin helped modernize the department and introduced the community policing concept, which "perceives the community as an agent and partner in promoting security rather than as a passive audience." During his tenure, he allowed his department to give technical advice for the first three seasons of the revived version of the Jack Webb-created detective drama, *Dragnet*, and he even made an appearance at the end of the Season Two finale, "The Big Problem," in a plea for improved community relations between the department and the city and during the first season of the police drama, *Adam-12*.[2]

Daryl Gates was the Chief of the Los Angeles Police Department from 1978 to 1992. His length of tenure was second only to that of William H. Parker. As Chief of Police, he took a hardline, aggressive, paramilitary approach to law enforcement. Gates is co-credited with creating SWAT teams with LAPD's John Nelson, who others claim was the originator of SWAT in 1965. Gates also co-founded D.A.R.E. along with the Los Angeles Unified School District. After the

Rodney King beating and the riots afterward, Gates retired from the police department. He was attributed with much of the blame.[3]

Then in recent years, there's been the release of FBI documents on Marilyn. Things that had been classified that we didn't have access to. Same as the CIA because both the FBI and the CIA watched her. She had attracted the interest of both of those agencies. So, I felt that someone had to put all of this together like a jigsaw puzzle. It's a great mystery, but can sense be made of it? And can we tell who the players are and who the actors are? Was Marilyn, in fact, murdered? I've concluded absolutely yes. No question that it was a contract killing. So, who was involved, and what can we learn about that? Years of research.

Q. On the previous show that we recorded, guest Jay Margolis claimed that RFK was behind the murder. I noticed that Milo Speriglio in *Crypt 33* seemed to have the same opinion. What is your opinion on that?

Milo A. Speriglio was a private detective hired to look into the death of Natalie Wood. But it was his involvement a few years later in the Marilyn Monroe death case that really put Speriglio on the map. Speriglio investigated Monroe's suicide for more than two decades and argued that she was the victim of a Chicago mob hit ordered by President John F. Kennedy's family members. He wrote three books on the subject. In *Crypt 33, The Saga Of Monroe*, Speriglio and another Los Angeles Private Investigator, Gregory Adela, recounted their evidence. At the age of 62, Milo died of lung cancer on April 30, 2000, at his home in Los Angeles.

A. Well, actually, let's take them one at a time. Let's talk about Milo first and *Crypt 33*. He talked about Bobby Kennedy's involvement with Marilyn. In fact, he claims she became pregnant by Bobby Kennedy, and there was an abortion in the months before her death. He had promised to get a divorce from Ethel and marry Marilyn. She became upset and threatened to become public about a lot of things. He never pointed the finger at Bobby Kennedy as being responsible for her death. But he certainly was a party interest.

Now, Margolis has a very good book. I disagree with parts of its conclusions. That's fine. You can pick and choose between us. I do not think that Bobby Kennedy was responsible for her death. I do believe that he was at her house that afternoon. We know from the housekeeper, from what she finally testified to, that there was quite an argument that day between them and that they both had become very upset.

But we know a lot more than that. And it makes us look in other directions for who did it. I know that Margolis placed a lot of emphasis on the testimony of the housekeeper's nephew. Her nephew, Norman Jeffries, I think his name was, had a lot of things to say years later. He claimed that Bobby Kennedy returned later that night with a couple of other people, and that was when Marilyn was murdered.

But if you want to go to *Crypt 33* again for a minute, he says no, and that it was a mob hit. He names the three hitmen as to who ordered it. Well, it was a mob hit, so it was ordered by Sam Giancana.

Samuel Mooney Giancana was an American mobster who was the boss of the Chicago Outfit from 1957 to 1966. According to some sources, Giancana and the Mafia were involved in John F. Kennedy's victory in the 1960 presidential election. During the 1960s, he was recruited by the Central Intelligence Agency in a plot to assassinate Cuban leader Fidel Castro. Conspiracy theorists consider Giancana, along with Mafia leaders Santo Trafficante Jr. and Carlos Marcello, associated with Kennedy's assassination. In 1965, Giancana was convicted of contempt of court, serving one year in prison. After his release from prison, Giancana fled to Cuernavaca, Mexico. In 1974, he was deported to the United States, returning to Chicago. Giancana was murdered on June 19, 1975, in Oak Park, Illinois, shortly before he was scheduled to appear before the Church Committee.[4]

I conclude this because there was a confession by close relatives of Sam Giancana who came forward in a book called *Double Cross* and said that Sam Giancana had confessed to them before he died. But he said that he was ordered at the behest of the CIA and that it was really a CIA contract to the mob.

Double Cross: The Explosive Inside Story of the Mobster Who Controlled America was written by mob boss Sam Giancana's brother Chuck Giancana, and nephew, also Sam. "According to the book, one of the most feared Chicago mobsters, Sam Giancana, clawed his way to the top of the Mafia hierarchy by starting as a hitman for Al Capone. He partied with major stars such as Frank Sinatra and Marilyn Monroe and did business with agents ranging from the CIA to the Vatican to the Shah of Iran. They also claim that the CIA asked Giancana to assassinate Fidel Castro. The book includes Giancana's testimony about the truth of his involvement in the deaths of Monroe and others. Chuck Giancana contributes a unique perspective of the mob's relationship with the Bay of Pigs and many other pivotal events of the 60s and beyond. *Double Cross* is an eye-opening account of the interworking of the government and the mob and how this relationship has impacted American history."[5]

They did that in those days. We know that. That's history that you can research. Check out the mob's involvement on behalf of the CIA in an attempt to assassinate Fidel Castro. Trujillo was assassinated. Look into those details, and you will see that the CIA used the "at arm's length" as a hit squad when they didn't want something traced back to them.

Rafael Leónidas Trujillo Molina, nicknamed "El Jefe," or "The Chief," or "The Boss," was a

Dominican dictator who ruled the Dominican Republic from February 1930 until his assassination in May 1961. On Tuesday, May 30, 1961, Trujillo was shot and killed when his blue 1957 Chevrolet Bel Air was ambushed on the road outside the Dominican capital. He was the victim of an ambush plotted by a number of men, such as General Juan Tomás Díaz, Pedro Livio Cedeño, Antonio de la Maza, Amado García Guerrero, and General Antonio Imbert Barrera. However, the plotters failed to take control as the later-executed General José René Román Fernandez betrayed his co-conspirators by his inactivity, and contingency plans had not been made. The role of the CIA in the killing has been debated. General Imbert Barrera insists that the plotters acted on their own. However, Trujillo was certainly murdered with weapons supplied by the CIA. In a 1975 report to the Deputy Attorney General of the United States, CIA officials described the agency as having no active part in the assassination and only a faint connection with the groups that planned the killing. However, the report is contradicted by later evidence.[6]

Now, was Giancana telling the truth? A CIA document surfaced signed by the head of counterintelligence, James Angleton, back in 1962. It matches very, very closely with the Sam Giancana confession.

James Jesus Angleton was chief of CIA Counterintelligence from 1954 to 1975. His official position within the organization was Associate Deputy Director of Operations for Counterintelligence. Angleton was significantly involved in the US response to the purported KGB defectors Anatoliy Golitsyn and Yuri Nosenko.[7]

As far as concern, Marilyn was going to go public about some things that were top secret that she wasn't supposed to know. That concern was there. These pieces link up in a way that I think Margolis hasn't put together. Now, who 's right?

Q. But wouldn't JFK know that he was sharing secrets with Marilyn that would threaten her life?

A. He was probably aware but careless. He had a lot of mistresses and a number of them he talked to. Mary Pinchot Meyer, a mistress for a long time, was assassinated a year after his death right when the Warren Commission Report was coming out. She knew too much.

Mary Eno Pinchot Meyer was an American painter who lived in Washington D.C. She was married to Central Intelligence Agency official Cord Meyer from 1945–1958 and became involved romantically with President John F. Kennedy after her divorce from Meyer. Pinchot Meyer was shot to death on the Chesapeake & Ohio Canal towpath on October 12, 1964. A suspect, Ray Crump, Jr., was arrested and charged with her murder but was ultimately acquitted. Pinchot Meyer's life, her relationship with Kennedy, and her murder have been the subjects of numerous articles and books.[8]

There was Judith Exner Campbell. She was
a go-between JFK and Sam Giancana
because they had business together. The
mob had helped put Kennedy in the White
House by delivering Chicago. Yet the
Kennedy administration, through Bobby
Kennedy, moved fiercely against the
mobsters and tried to put them behind
bars.

Judith Exner was an American woman who
claimed to be the mistress of U.S. president John F.
Kennedy and Mafia leaders Sam Giancana and John
Roselli. She was also known as Judith Campbell
Exner and Judith Campbell. In 1977, Exner
published *Judith Exner: My Story*. In her memoir,
she said that her relationship with Kennedy was
entirely personal. She also said that Frank Sinatra
later introduced her to Sam Giancana, with whom
she also became intimate. She said that Giancana
never asked her for any information related to
Kennedy. She also said that John Roselli was her
friend. In 1997, Exner alleged more details and
changed her story, in separate interviews with Liz

Smith of *Vanity Fair* and Seymour Hersh. She said Kennedy told her of his plans related to Cuba and used her to carry money to Giancana, as well as to arrange numerous meetings between him, Giancana, and Roselli. She claimed to Smith to have terminated a pregnancy resulting from the last encounter in 1962 with Kennedy. She said that she had carried payoffs from California defense contractors to the Kennedys, including Robert F. Kennedy. A witness of Hersh's who appeared to support Exner's story of carrying money to Giancana later dropped his story. Judith Campbell Exner lived in Newport Beach and was a painter. She died on September 24, 1999, in Duarte, California, from breast cancer.[9]

That's why the Giancana's, the family, has said that the murder was timed, intended to be entrapment of Bobby Kennedy. They were trying to solve two problems at once.

On the one hand, they had been asked to eliminate Marilyn Monroe because of the problems she presented to the CIA from her knowledge of classified things and concerned that she was getting ready to talk. On the other hand, because they had wiretaps, they knew that Bobby Kennedy was there that day. There's another reason they may have known he was there that afternoon too. Bobby Kennedy was staying at that time with a lawyer, who had been a lawyer for Sam Giancana. He represented the mob. He represented Sam Giancana during the Senate crime hearings. You can look at the old newsreels, and you'll see it's the same guy.

So, Bobby Kennedy was with him, and he takes off for Los Angeles. We don't know the extent of loyalties, disloyalty, treachery, who told what. We do know for sure that there were wiretaps, and the mob felt that, according to the Giancana family, if they struck then, the day after Bobby Kennedy had been there, then the police investigation would come up with his fingerprints. The investigation would show letters; maybe there would even be a diary. There would be things that would tie her to the Kennedys. The mob felt it would help bring the Kennedys down. That's what they wanted.

I agree with probably 95 percent of the Margolis book, except for their conclusion that Bobby Kennedy was actually involved with murdering her. I do not think that was the case.

Q. So, you said that not only did the CIA and FBI have Marilyn bugged, but Jimmy Hoffa did as well. Why would Hoffa have her house bugged?

A. That's a really good question. I have testimony from the wiretap guys, and one of them, Fred Otash, did the dirty work. He bugged her house when she was on a trip to Mexico. He also planted bugs at Peter Lawford's Malibu estate. Peter Lawford was a brother-in-law of JFK. They had big parties there. We think it may have been at one of those parties that JFK first met Marilyn Monroe. He was working on behalf of Hoffa and Sam Giancana. Hoffa was head of the teamsters, and they were deep in the mob's pockets as far as money. The early casinos were built in Las Vegas with heavy mob participation and the teamster's pension fund. I don't know if it was legal or illegal that the pension fund went into the hands of those who were building the casinos. So, they were all in bed together.

Fred Otash was a Los Angeles police officer, private investigator, author, and a WWII Marine veteran, who became known as a Hollywood fixer while operating as its most infamous private detective. He is most remembered as the inspiration for Jack Nicholson's character, Jake Gittes, in the film *Chinatown*. Otash worked for Hollywood Research Incorporated, which did business with the tabloid magazine *Confidential*. He was also known for being hired by Peter Lawford to investigate Marilyn Monroe. An FBI file released as part of the JFK Assassination Records suggests that Otash was investigating Lawford and John F. Kennedy and attempted to talk a call-girl into arranging a meeting with Kennedy in which she would wear a wire to record incriminating statements. Otash also was involved in the investigation of the "Wrong Door

Raid" involving Frank Sinatra. Otash wrote about his life in his memoir, *Investigation Hollywood: Memoirs Of Hollywood's Top Private Detective*.[10]

Hoffa hated the Kennedys and Robert Kennedy as Attorney General. Same as Sam Giancana. Once Marilyn became a sort of plaything of the Kennedys, first JFK and later Bobby, sure they wanted to wiretap her. They were looking for anything they could find to use against JFK and bring him down. In the end, they all got theirs. Jimmy Hoffa, you know he disappeared. Nobody found the body. In the case of Sam Giancana, it was eight bullets. Most of them to the head in his own home, assassinated. So, everybody got paid back in the end.

Q. There was a large fear of communism in America in the 1960s, and Marilyn actually had a tie to the communists as well, correct?

A. She walked right into the middle of it. First of all, let me say a little about

Marilyn's background here. She was an orphan, her mother was still alive, but she grew up in an orphanage because her mother was psychologically incapable, and her mother was institutionalized. So, for all intents and purposes, she was an orphan. She went from foster home to foster home and was very, very poor. She had nothing in her early years, so she identified with under tribe. Some of the books she read were written by communists.

The other thing was she was very sympathetic to integration and the plight of the blacks. In those days in America, there was a big push in favor of integration and equal rights for blacks from the American Communist Party. The big point of departure for her was when she married Arthur Miller. He was a great playwright and wrote *Death of a Salesman*. You could say that he was either a communist, or he had communist leanings. In those days, there was a House on American Un-Activities Committee and Senator Joseph McCarthy and the witch hunt against any American citizens who had ties to the

Communist Party, Russia, and Russian communism.

The House Un-American Activities Committee (HUAC) – from 1969 onwards, known as the House Committee on Internal Security, was an investigative committee of the United States House of Representatives. The HUAC was created in 1938 to investigate alleged disloyalty and subversive activities on the part of private citizens, public employees, and those organizations suspected of having fascist or communist ties. The committee's anti-communist investigations are often compared to and confused with those of Joseph McCarthy, who, as a U.S. Senator, had no direct involvement with the House committee. McCarthy was the chairman of the Government Operations Committee and its Permanent Subcommittee on Investigations of the U.S. Senate, not the House.

In 1947, the committee held nine days of hearings into alleged communist propaganda and influence in the Hollywood motion picture industry. After conviction on contempt of Congress charges for refusal to answer some questions posed by committee members, "The Hollywood Ten" were blacklisted by the industry. Eventually, more than 300 artists, including directors, radio commentators, actors, and particularly screenwriters, were boycotted by the studios. Some, like Charlie Chaplin, Orson Welles, Alan Lomax, Paul Robeson, and Yip Harburg, left the U.S or went underground to find work. Others like Dalton Trumbo wrote under pseudonyms or the names of colleagues. Only about ten percent succeeded in rebuilding careers within the entertainment industry.

When the House abolished the committee in 1975, its functions were transferred to the House Judiciary Committee.[11]

So, many people from Hollywood were called to testify in front of the House of Un-American Activities. Those who refused to name names, well, some of them went to jail. It was a crime not to cooperate with the committee. Arthur Miller, who had recently married Marilyn Monroe, at that point was called before the committee and was considered uncooperative. So, at that

point, you had not only people like Hoffa
and Giancana interested in wiretapping
Marilyn Monroe but certainly the FBI.
Especially so when she went to Mexico to
visit a Vanderbilt heir, who was a
communist. Then the CIA got involved in
watching her, too, because the CIA's
jurisdiction is espionage outside the United
States. She became a person of interest to
all of these Government agencies, and she
was in the thick of it but didn't know it.
She really didn't know what deep water she
was in. She was a bit naïve about it. It set
up the circumstances where she became a
serious target.

Q. Was her husband Arthur Miller
blackballed from working too?

A. Good question. I know that the House of
Un-American Activities censured him,
which was really bad news but then they
took it back. I don't know. He made some
concessions. It was decided that he had not
committed a criminal offense by refusing to
give them whatever information that they
wanted. He was not censured like other

writers. One of his scripts called *The Misfits*, directed by John Huston, starred Marilyn Monroe, even though they were getting divorced at that time. They made his movie with his name on it. But there were other writers that couldn't work under their real names. They had to write all of their things anonymously. They would use a different name and get paid under the table. But her marriage to Arthur Miller was certainly a huge set back to her personal safety, if not her career.

"Playwright Arthur Miller defies the House Committee on Un-American Activities and refuses to name suspected communists."[12] When Miller attended the HUAC hearing, to which Monroe accompanied him, risking her own career, he gave the committee a detailed account of his political activities. Reneging on the chairman's promise, the committee demanded the names of friends and colleagues who had participated in similar activities. Miller refused to comply, saying, "I could not use the name of another person and bring trouble on him."As a result, a judge found

312 CONSPIRACY THEORY CULTURE

Miller guilty of contempt of Congress in May 1957. Miller was sentenced to a fine and a prison sentence, blacklisted. His passport had already been denied when he tried to go to Brussels to attend the premiere of his play, *The Crucible*, about the Salem witch trials. In August 1958, his conviction was overturned by the court of appeals, which ruled that Miller had been misled by the chairman of the HUAC.[13]

Q. The last person to speak to Marilyn was Jose Bolanos?

A. Jose Bolanos claimed he was the last to talk with her. He has what I think is a very consistent story that held up, and he was extensively interviewed.

Jose Bolaños was born in Mexico City in 1935 and died there on June 11, 1994. He was known as something of a playboy but was also a screenwriter and director. He married Italian actress Venetia Vianello, but his biggest claim to fame is his relationship with Marilyn Monroe.[14]

But the mainstream people think that Peter Lawford was the last one to talk with her. Bolanos said that he had been her escort to the Golden Globes Awards that year. She had met him on a trip to Mexico. He was a Mexican screenwriter, quite handsome. He said that he was in Los Angeles that night and had called her. They were talking on the phone, and there had been some commotion at the door. She put down the phone and never returned. He said that something was going on in the background, that someone came in, and the phone just clicked.

The other key thing he said, I think, is that she said she knew a secret from the President that was so big it would change the whole world one day. He didn't ever admit if she did tell him what that secret was. But since he had that conversation, in an interview may have been with Donald Wolfe years later, you have to ask yourself what was that secret at that time in 1962, that would still have been secret by the time this interview happened.

That gets us to things like the "Roswell" case. I'm interested in that because, as you mentioned, I was the producer of Showtime's movie *Roswell* and the controversy about what happened in Roswell in 1947. The military announced that they recovered a crashed flying saucer. Then they changed the story and said it was a weather balloon.

In the CIA document that I mentioned with James Angleton's signature, which we are really sure is a legitimate bonafide document for many reasons, it charted the contents of a wire conversation that Marilyn's friend Dorothy Kilgallen had with a Marilyn associate in New York. Some of the things that Marilyn had been told about by JFK came out in that wiretap. One of them was a visit to a secret airbase by John F. Kennedy for the purpose of examining things from outer space. It said that in the CIA document, and Dorothy Kilgallen speculated that it had to do with the downed flying saucer in that case, which would have been Roswell.

Dorothy Mae Kilgallen was an American journalist and television game show panelist. In 1938, she began her newspaper column, *The Voice of Broadway*, which eventually was syndicated to more than 140 papers. Kilgallen's columns featured mostly show business news and gossip but ventured into other topics, such as politics and organized crime. She wrote front-page articles on the Sam Sheppard trial and later the John F. Kennedy assassination. On November 8, 1965, Kilgallen was found dead in her Manhattan townhouse located at 45 East 68th Street. Her death was determined to have been caused by a fatal combination of alcohol and barbiturates. Several authors have claimed that she was murdered to prevent her from revealing a conspiracy to assassinate John F. Kennedy.[15]

Q. How do you feel about Roswell being the secret that Marilyn knew about because Kennedy told her?

A. Well, to make the movie *Roswell* I did extensive research, and I was involved with those who were doing great in-depth research at that time. One of them, Kevin

Randle, who's just come out with a new book, *Roswell for the 21st Century*, has backed off in his certainty of it being extra-terrestrial.

I don't view kindly to what they call his recanting because I know some of the things he was told at that time, from, for example, the Provost Marshal, who was head of the Military Police that recovered the debris from the field. The debris that Intelligence Officer, Jessie Marcell, said in 1986, "Was not made on this Earth, and it couldn't have been."

I believe that all of the current theories are wrong. They are either deliberate disinformation or are mistaken. It was extra-terrestrial contact. There's so much good testimony from solid people about it who were there at that time.

I think because the Marilyn Monroe document, signed by the head of counterintelligence, mentions JFK's visit to a secret airbase for the purpose of examining things from outer space, I can agree with what Dorothy Kilgallen referred to as the downed flying saucer from outer space of the southwest in 1947.

I think all of these pieces historically interlock. One more point, how do we know that the CIA document is real? Some have said that it was a forgery. Well, no, it turns out that author Don Burleson went through the Freedom of Information Act procedures on that to look through the CIA transcripts of the wiretap referred to in that document. However, the first search by the CIA said that they hadn't found any transcripts. But you can appeal that if you want to. He appealed it through the proper procedures, and the CIA accepted his appeal of their original denial. He quite rightly pointed out that the CIA would have never accepted an appeal based on a document that was fraudulent or wasn't theirs.

Q. Most people believe that Marilyn died of an overdose either on purpose or by accident. How do you think that Marilyn died?

A. Well, the Giancana family claims that it was a suppository injection of the drugs she was taking. That jives with part of the autopsy report that talked about this purplish discoloration of the colon that was never satisfactorily explained. So, that's consistent.

The thing that isn't consistent with the idea that she swallowed a lot of pills was that no water glass was ever found in the room where her body was found. How did she take those pills? Some of the research indicated that the toxicity level of her blood was so high, so massive, that she would have died before taking that many pills. In other words, she would have been dead en route to get there in order for her blood toxicity to go there. There was none of the crystalline residue, usually found in cases like that, found in her stomach. Some researchers have tried to bring science into it and say, no, the stomach acids could have theoretically dissolved those capsules. Theoretically, it would have been possible, but they didn't see the residue.

The first policeman who came to the scene and discovered her, Sargent Jack Clemmons, was suspicious from the beginning saying, "It didn't look like a suicide. It looked like it was staged to look like a suicide." He has seen overdose victims before, and there was always vomit, but none in this case. The body is always contorted, but in this case, the body was just laid out perfectly as though it was posed.

Police Chief Tom Reddin said that it was handled like a top-secret intelligence operation in the hours after her death because of the Attorney General of the United States. I think what he meant was that it was kept secret to try to protect Bobby Kennedy. He was vulnerable in that situation. He was with her. He was in town, and he had an argument with her. They got him out of town. They spent five or six hours after her body was discovered before it was officially reported to Sargent Jack Clemmons, a low-level sergeant at the police department. But higher-level operatives had been working on cleaning up the scene for hours. That's why Marilyn looked staged to Sergeant Clemmons when he got there.

Bottom line – it was covered up. We were lied to. She didn't commit suicide. It was a contract killing. It was a terrible episode in American history. It's kind of presaged the violence that was to come. It was one year, approximately before the assassination of President Kennedy, that Marilyn was the result of a contract killing.

The first allegations that Marilyn had been murdered originated in anti-communist activist Frank A. Capell's self-published pamphlet, *The Strange Death of Marilyn Monroe 1964*, in which he claimed that her death was part of a communist conspiracy. He claimed that Monroe and U.S. Attorney General Robert F. Kennedy had an affair, which she took too seriously and was threatening to cause a scandal. Kennedy ordered her to be assassinated to protect his career. In addition to accusing Kennedy of being a communist sympathizer, Capell also claimed that many other people close to Monroe, such as her doctors and ex-husband Arthur Miller, were communists. Capell's credibility has been seriously questioned because his only source was columnist Walter Winchell, who in turn had received much of his information from Capell, therefore, was citing himself.

His friend, LAPD Sergeant Jack Clemmons, aided him in developing his pamphlet. Clemmons became a central source for conspiracy theorists. He was the first Police Officer on the scene of Monroe's death and later made claims that he had not mentioned in the official 1962 investigation that when he arrived at Monroe's house, her housekeeper was washing her sheets, and he had a sixth sense that something was wrong.

Capell and Clemmons' allegations have been linked to their political goals. Capell dedicated his life to revealing an "International Communist Conspiracy," and Clemmons was a member of The Police and Fire Research Organization (FiPo), which sought to expose "subversive activities which threaten our American way of life." FiPo and similar organizations were known for their stance against the Kennedys and for sending the Federal Bureau of Investigation letters incriminating them. The 1964 FBI file that speculated on an affair between Monroe and Robert F. Kennedy is likely to have come from them.

Furthermore, Capell, Clemmons, and a third person were indicted in 1965 by a California grand jury for conspiracy to libel by obtaining and distributing a false affidavit. They claimed that Senator Thomas Kuchel had once been arrested for a homosexual act. They had done this because Kuchel had supported the Civil Rights Act of 1964. Capell pleaded guilty, and charges against Clemmons were dropped after he resigned from the LAPD.[16]

Listen to the full interview with Paul Davids on my website:

houseofmysteryradio/episodes/paul-davids-marilyn-declassified

Interview Afterthoughts

I always heard rumors that perhaps Marilyn Monroe didn't kill herself, and that she was murdered, but never heard any reasons why. So, having the radio show, this was a perfect way to jump in and find out if and why she would have been murdered.

I actually interviewed several people that either wrote books or made a documentary about the subject and selected what I thought to be the most credible of those. Most of them all had the same cause of her murder, and there were two main suspects of the murder, The Kennedy brothers, or the deep state of the government through either the CIA or FBI.

The basic premise of Marilyn being murdered was that after she ended her affair with John F. Kennedy, she soon moved onto sleeping with his brother , Robert Kennedy. The two Kennedy's were very powerful people in the early 60's, John being president, and Robert being the Attorney General.

This apparently led the CIA, FBI, and even the Mafia and Jimmy Hoffa to bug her house, so that they could listen in on her affair with Bobby and maybe get some dirt of the Kennedy's. This sounds kind of logical especially in today's suspicious world, but was it true?

The biggest problem with this theory is we only have a few witnesses to these tapes of both Kennedy's and other powerful people interacting with Monroe in her house. Therefore, we have to believe in what they say that they heard on these recordings, and even if you believe that they are reliable people, you have to trust their memories as well.

The claim about what was heard on these recordings was that Marilyn had become pregnant with Bobby Kennedy's child. This was supposed to have really upset Kennedy, and the two of them got into a large fight the night before she died. Some say that she was threatening to expose her affairs and pregnancy to the press, and so Robert Kennedy had to kill her to stop it.

The other major claim brought up about her death is the amount of sleeping pills that she had in her house. From what the claimed autopsy report says, she would have had to have more pills in her system than she had available at her home, or by the prescriptions she had filled previously. They even say that she would have been dead before she could have swallowed that many pills.

These sound like great storylines for a great crime fiction novel, but there is no evidence of anything that's been claimed. The only thing that we know for sure is that Marilyn Monroe had an addiction sleeping pills and alcohol, and she died with too much of them in her system.

There was no proof of her being pregnant, or even having an abortion before she had died. In fact, there's nothing to establish that she even had an affair with Robert Kennedy, other than gossip. Quite a few of the writers behind her death being a murder, say that she was in a happy time of her life, and was about to remarry and go back to filming movies for 1 million dollars.

We have absolutely no evidence of any of this. Truth is she was failing in her career, had been fired, and recently divorced from her last husband.

Bottom line: Celebrity deaths such as Marilyn Monroe captivates the world, people love to hear the salacious details of a famous person's life, and how it went wrong. Perhaps it makes us feel better about our normal lives. All of the books and movies made about her death, all center around the possible motives for some people or government agencies to want to kill her, but no evidence.

---

1. *Marilyn Monroe: Declassified* | Online Video | SBS Movies. https://www.sbs.com.au/movies/video/869149251582/ Marilyn-Monroe-Declassified
2. https://en.wikipedia.org/wiki/Thomas_Reddin
3. https://en.wikipedia.org/wiki/Daryl_Gates
4. https://en.wikipedia.org/wiki/Sam_Giancana
5. https://www.simonandschuster.com/books/Double-Cross/Sam-Giancana/9781510711259
6. https://en.wikipedia.org/wiki/Rafael_Trujillo
7. https://en.wikipedia.org/wiki/James_Jesus_Angleton
8. https://en.wikipedia.org/wiki/Mary_Pinchot_Meyer
9. https://en.wikipedia.org/wiki/Judith_Exner
10. https://en.wikipedia.org/wiki/Fred_Otash
11. https://en.wikipedia.org/wiki/House_Un-American_Activities_Committee
12. https://www.history.com/this-day-in-history/arthur-miller-refuses-to-name-communists
13. https://www.litlovers.com/reading-guides/fiction/8674-death-of-a-salesman-miller?start=1
14. https://www.imdb.com/name/nm0049443/bio?ref_=nm_ov_bio_sm
15. https://en.wikipedia.org/wiki/Dorothy_Kilgallen
16. https://en.wikipedia.org/wiki/Death_of_Marilyn_Monroe

Princess Diana was Murdered

∽❀∾

The Conspiracy Theory

By 2013, with the surge of self-published books, magazines, and internet blogs, a lot of writers just started saying whatever they thought without any evidence at all. Now, there was one less screening process on written works – the publisher. Publishers used to screen their books and check facts before publishing them, so they would not get sued for publishing misinformation.

With the new self-publishing boom, that fact-checking process was now gone. Writers were beginning to publish things based completely on their feelings, and because they believed so much in their theory, they sometimes created evidence. Unfortunately, this started to become a mainstream theme online, and people started to believe the lies.

These next two authors are a perfect example of this. Both were interviewed and given a chance to explain their reasons why they believe Princess Diana was murdered instead of simply dying in a tragic car accident.

Within two months of Alan Power releasing his book on Princess Diana, John Morgan published a book calling Power's book all lies. Power's response was to think that perhaps the MI6 or the British establishment was behind Morgan's book.

Interview with John Morgan

John Morgan, who is based in Brisbane, Australia, is an investigative writer with a diploma in journalism. Since 2005, he has carried out extensive full-time research into the events surrounding the deaths of Diana, Princess of Wales, and Dodi Fayed. John viewed it as a huge injustice to the memory of Princess Diana.

The 2007 book, *Cover-up of a Royal Murder*, was the result of his subsequent investigation into the "Paget Report," documenting the 2007 inquest the jury had prevented the public from seeing. The *Diana Inquest* series of books is the result of his thorough research and investigation into the facts of the case.

John went on to closely follow and analyze the proceedings and transcripts of the London inquest into the deaths of Princess Diana and Dodi Fayed. In 2010, he received over 500 documents from within the official British police investigation, Operation Paget.

The John Morgan interview was in 2014.

Q. How did you get interested in the death of Princess Diana?

A. I got interested in the case of Princess Diana after there was a letter published in 2003, which was a note from Diana to her butler, that predicted she could die in an orchestrated car crash. I saw that handwritten note, which was published in the newspapers all around the world, and within two years, she actually did die as she predicted in the letter.

The Princess of Wales wrote to her former butler, Paul Burrell, saying her life was at its "most dangerous" phase, the *Daily Mirror* reported. It quotes the letter as saying: "XXXX is planning 'an accident' in my car, brake failure and serious head injury in order to make the path clear for Charles to marry."[1]

That was a very significant piece of evidence, I thought. In 2006, I retired and decided I could write a book and decided I would do a bit of research on that crash. In 2006, when the police investigation was completed in December of 2006, I had already done about 18 months of research on what had taken place.

After the police report was put online, I printed out all 800 pages and read it. I then realized that the police investigation had not really been an investigation and appeared to be more interested in trying to cover it up. There were so many errors in that report as I already knew a lot about it.

The police investigation finished in December of 2006, and the inquest started ten months later in October 2007. During that time, I published a book about the police report, and Mohamed Al-Fayed distributed it to the lawyers at the inquest. I got feedback from a lot of the lawyers who said they used the book in the inquest.

Mohamed Al-Fayed is an Egyptian-born businessman whose residence and chief business interests have been in the United Kingdom since the late 1960s. Fayed's business interests include ownership of Hôtel Ritz Paris and formerly Harrods Department Store. Fayed famously had a son, Dodi, from his first marriage to Samira Khashoggi from 1954 to 1956. Dodi was in a romantic relationship with Diana, Princess of Wales, when they both died in a car crash in Paris in 1997.

From February 1998, Al-Fayed maintained that the crash was a result of a conspiracy and later contended that the crash was orchestrated by MI6 on the instructions of Prince Philip, Duke of Edinburgh.[2]

Al-Fayed first claimed that the Princess was pregnant to the *Daily Express* in May 2001 and that he was the only person who had been told of this news. Witnesses at the inquest who said the Princess was not pregnant, and could not have been, were part of the conspiracy, according to Al-Fayed.

Fayed's testimony at the inquest was roundly condemned in the press as being farcical. Members of the British Government's Intelligence and Security Committee accused Fayed of turning the inquest into a 'circus' and called for it to be ended maturely. Lawyers representing Al-Fayed later accepted at the inquest that there was no direct evidence that either the Duke of Edinburgh or MI6 had been involved in any murder conspiracy involving Diana or Dodi. His claims that the crash was a result of a conspiracy were dismissed by a French judicial investigation, but Fayed appealed against this verdict. The British "Operation Paget," a Metropolitan police inquiry that concluded in 2006, also found no evidence of a conspiracy. To Al-Fayed made 175 conspiracy claims. In 2013, Fayed's wealth was estimated at US$1.4 billion, making him the 1,031st richest person in the world.[3]

As the transcripts of the inquest came out, I would read through and study them, and I wrote a series of six volumes based on what was in the inquest transcripts, but also the police reports. In 2010, I received a huge batch of documents that were from the British police investigation, and there were very critical documents about the case, and none of them had been shown to the jury at the inquest. I published a lot of those documents, including the post-mortem reports for Princess Diana and Dodi Fayed, none of which were shown to the jury either while investigating the cause of death. One of the things that's very interesting is that the verdict of that inquest jury was quite different from what the police investigation had concluded.

Dodi Fayed was an Egyptian film producer and the son of billionaire Mohamed Al-Fayed. He was the romantic partner of Diana, Princess of Wales, when they both died in a car crash in Paris in 1997. In July 1997, Fayed became romantically involved with Diana, Princess of Wales. Earlier that summer, Fayed had become engaged to an American model, Kelly Fisher, and had bought a house in Malibu, California, for himself and Fisher with money from his father. Fisher subsequently claimed Fayed had jilted her for Diana and announced that she was filing a breach of contract suit against him, claiming he had led her emotionally all the way up to the altar and abandoned her when they were almost there. He threw her love away in a callous way with no regard for her whatsoever. She dropped the lawsuit shortly after Fayed's death.[4]

Naturally, there was a French police investigation that started on the day of the crash. In 1999, they produced their results that stated the crash was caused by the driver, Henri Paul, who was drunk. The British police investigation that came out in

2006 also said that it was caused by the driver, Henri Paul, who was drunk and speeding. So, it was a very similar finding to the French investigation.

But the inquest jury's verdict was quite different. It was unlawful killing by the driver of the Mercedes, Henri Paul, but also by unknown following vehicles, which have not been identified. But they were not paparazzi. So, quite different from what the police had concluded.

Henri Paul was the driver of the Mercedes W140, in which Diana, Princess of Wales, died on August 31, 1997. As Deputy Head of Security at the Hôtel Ritz Paris, Paul had been off duty that evening but was called back to drive Diana and Dodi Fayed to their apartment. The car crashed at high speed in the Pont de l'Alma tunnel, with only bodyguard Trevor Rees-Jones surviving. British and French police investigations put the blame largely on Paul for being impaired by alcohol and later driving recklessly.

On the night of August 31, 1997, Paul was under the influence of alcohol and tried to elude paparazzi photographers at high speed estimated at over double the 50 kilometers per hour speed limit, when the Mercedes S280 he was driving crashed into a column supporting the Pont de l'Alma tunnel in Paris. Paul's blood alcohol content level was subsequently found to be between 1.73 g/L and 1.75 g/L or 0.17% mass/vol. A figure more than three times the threshold for drunk driving as defined under French law. Paul's parents dispute the authenticity and the accuracy of the test results, as does Dodi's father, Mohamed Al-Fayed. There have been many conspiracy theories surrounding the car crash.[5]

The establishment didn't really get it past the jury, even though the true finding would have been murder. The jury was not unanimous. It was 9-2. There were two jurors who did not conclude unlawful killing. They concluded murder.

French Investigation

Friends of Henri Paul testified in statements to the French police that he did not have a remarkably high tolerance for alcohol and was seen on social occasions to drink for several hours while showing obvious signs of drunkenness. In her statement to French police, his medical doctor, Dominique Mélo, who was also a friend, explained: "Henri drank like everyone else, but not to excess. He did not have the clinical stigmata or the behavior of a chronic alcoholic," she explained further.

Paul's doctor testified that in the two years leading up to his death, he had depressive episodes about the break-up of a long-term relationship and had sometimes taken to drinking at home outside a social context. She believed he was not alcohol-dependent, but she was worried that he might become so, and in about June 1996, she prescribed him the anti-depressant Prozac and an anti-alcoholism medication Aotal. Traces of the anti-depressants were found in post-mortem examinations of his blood. The inquest revealed that the autopsy also found Paul's liver to be normal with no indicating signs of problems connected with alcoholism.[6]

British Investigation

Operation Paget investigated the reliability of the post-mortem examinations using DNA comparison of the disputed blood sample by comparing a DNA profile from it with Paul's mother's DNA profile. The test produced a result that there was a maternal relationship between the two profiles to a probability of 99.9997%. The level of carbon monoxide in this blood sample was attributed to the area of the body it was taken from, to his living in a built-up urban area, and smoking of small cigars in the hours leading up to his death.

It was disclosed that in November 2006, John Stevens had a meeting with Paul's parents and told them that their son was not drunk and was found to have indisputably had two alcoholic drinks. This was verified by bodyguards Trevor Rees-Jones and Kieran Wingfield, two barmen in the bar, the till records from the hotel bar, and a drink bill. Five weeks later, the report stated that Paul was twice over the British drink-drive limit and three times over the French limit.

An expert cited in the report estimated that Paul had drunk the equivalent of ten small glasses of

Ricard pastis, his favorite aperitif, before driving. At the British inquest in February 2008, Stevens denied "deliberately misleading" Paul's parents and explained the apparent contradiction in his statements by saying that Paul did not meet the standard definition of being drunk, which is dependent on observable physical behavior. He was though clearly "under the influence" of alcohol and unfit to drive.

An unexplained prescription-only drug called albendazole used to treat worm infestations was also found in hair samples from Paul. This drug is said to be commonly given to homeless people living on the streets. Paul's doctor denies prescribing this drug to Paul.

Q. So, are you saying that the police covered up that it was murder? Or, are you saying that it was just really bad police work?

A. No, it was intentionally covered up. One of the things was if you studied how the investigation was done, there are elements of them trying to find the truth. I think it was lower-level officers who were working on the case. Some of them were genuine in interviewing witnesses and were trying to establish what happened.

But yes, the police at the top was covering up, so they had to reach a conclusion that it was not murder. It's interesting, there's the stuff that indicates murder, and they drew these conclusions that it was an accident. It was quite easy when I did this book to show, well, that this evidence indicates murder. Yet they conclude it was an accident, a contradiction to what the evidence was. Very strange.

Q. How were the police and other officials towards you when you were investigating this case?

A. I haven't had any direct overtures from the establishment or against me. There was a lot of indirect stuff on the internet, but nothing direct. Nobody has given me a death threat or anything like that.

Q. Do you think the car accident was planned out ahead of time?

A. Yeah, it was a planned operation. Diana was under surveillance, so they were monitoring her when she was traveling around with Dodi and various trips that she was making. There was a phone call that Dodi made to the Ritz in Paris, which was owned by his father, on the 18th of August 1997. So, that was two weeks before. During that phone call, it was clear from anyone monitoring it that there was no doubt Dodi's phone calls were being monitored as well as Diana's. But there was a very clear statement that they would be traveling to Paris at the end of August.

So, basically, anyone that was part of the operation, which would have been units of the M16, would have been aware that the couple would be traveling to Paris at the end of August. And they had two weeks to organize the details of what they were going to do. It was an extremely well-planned operation. I think it was done with the help of the French intelligence and also the CIA. You can see the units are planning right through the operation. They knew in advance what they were going to do to cover it up – things like nailing it on the paparazzi and also on the drunk driver.

If you walked down the streets of London and asked people, "Who killed Diana," a lot of people would say the paparazzi. The other thing they might say is the driver because he was drunk. So, there are just two things in most people's minds, and they are both erroneous.

But these things were worked out before the crash, and you can see the evidence of it. Things like Henri Paul, who was working for intelligence, had no idea of what he was involved in. He had no idea that they were about to kill Diana. He probably thought the things he was doing was helping to protect her. One of the things and he was paid very well as there was a lot of money that went into his account, was Henri Paul acting as head of security for the hotel. The hotel was trying to secure the well-being of the guests, and Diana and Dodi were VIP guests. Yet Henri Paul was going out to the paparazzi and telling them when they were going to be coming out. He made about five trips in total out to the paparazzi, telling them, "They're not going to be very long."

So, why does anyone do that? It wasn't for the interest of the couple as they didn't want to be hounded by the paparazzi. The reason he was doing it was to make sure the paparazzi didn't go home as it was getting towards midnight, and they might have thought that the couple was just staying overnight, so there was no point in waiting outside. He was making sure that the paparazzi were staying, and he was getting paid to do that. That's why when the couple left the hotel, the paparazzi were still there, and they followed the Mercedes. They were on scooters and small cars, and they began the chase.

Once they got onto the expressway and heading towards the tunnel, they practically had no chance of keeping up. The witnesses who saw what happened on the expressway all say they saw several motorbikes surrounding the Mercedes. These were large dark motorbikes, and a couple of them had two passengers on them. The motorbikes were also taking flash photos as the car headed toward the tunnel. Basically, what I call "fake paparazzi." They were pretending to be paparazzi. So this was the whole thing, people that saw the motorbikes probably thought paparazzi as well. Then you've got to ask who was driving the motorbikes. None of the drivers on the motorbikes have been identified.

Even though the jury decided that there was unlawful chase by the motorbikes, when the inquest was completed, there was no attempt by any of the authorities in France or England to establish the identity of those motorbike riders.

They had been forced into the crash through surrounding motorbikes, and there was also a flash strobe light to the driver in the tunnel. If that were a normal person that this was done to, those motorbikes were the cause of the crash and unidentified, immediately following there would be a police investigation to establish who those motorbike riders were. That never occurred, as it's all part of the coverup.

Q. Was there a detail there that was assigned to protect Diana?

A. The royals do, but Diana wasn't a royal at the time, as she had been removed from the royal family a year earlier. Even when she was a royal in 1994, she had requested that her guard be withdrawn. She was no longer under day-to-day bodyguard protection from the police.

Q. You talk about the post-crash medical treatment of Diana. What's your opinion of it?

A. She survived the crash. So, when the crash occurred, it crashed under the third pillar of the tunnel at 60 miles an hour. The two people who were on the driver's side, Henri Paul, the driver in the front, and Dodi Fayed, the passenger sitting behind him in the back, both died instantly. The

> two people on the passenger side, Trevor
> Rees-Jones, the bodyguard was in the front,
> he's still alive, and Princess Diana in the
> back. She initially survived. Both of those
> people on the passenger side survived.

Trevor Rees-Jones is a German-born British bodyguard of Princess Diana. On August 31, 1997, Rees-Jones was seriously injured in the crash that resulted in the death of Diana, Princess of Wales. The Princess's boyfriend, Dodi Fayed, and the driver of the car, Henri Paul, were pronounced dead at the scene. Rees-Jones was the only survivor. Rees suffered severe brain and chest injuries, and every bone in his face was broken. He spent ten days in a coma. His face was reconstructed from family photographs by maxillofacial surgeon Luc Chikhani, using about 150 pieces of titanium to hold the bones together and recreate the original shape. Within a year, his face was nearly back to normal. Hospital care costs were paid by Dodi's father, Mohamed Al-Fayed, Rees-Jones's employer at the time of the crash, and the rest by the British National Health Service.

At first, it was widely rumored that Rees-Jones had lost his tongue in the crash, but this was untrue. He underwent a 10-hour operation to restore his jaw to a normal condition. Rees-Jones returned to Britain on October 3, 1997, having spent a month in the hospital. At the time, he was able to communicate only by whispering and writing down answers. He resigned from his job as a bodyguard on May 19, 1998. Al-Fayed was reported as saying that his job would be available if he wished to return.

Rees-Jones wrote a book, published in 2000 and titled *The Bodyguard's Story: Diana, the Crash, and the Sole Survivor*, about his experiences, with the help of ghostwriter Moira Johnston. The book reconstructed the events from Rees-Jones's partial memories and those of his family and friends. He decided to write the book because many bizarre stories had circulated about the crash and because his former employer, Al-Fayed, had accused him of not doing his job properly.[7]

The ambulance and the medical treatment are really the things that took her life.

Immediately after the crash at 12:21 a.m., there were two doctors that ran the base overnight. One of them was asleep, and the other one was Doctor Arnaud Derossi, who was taking the calls. He allocated an ambulance to the crash, which was Doctor Jean-Marc Martino, who didn't arrive until 12:47 a.m. However, the hospital he was dispatched from was only 2.3 kilometers away. So, he took a hell of a long time to get to the crash. It took 13 minutes to travel 2.3 kilometers.

Intelligence agencies use people as agents to do their work. They use people from all sorts of walks of life. People can have their career as a doctor, but they could also be working as an agent. It could be your next-door neighbor. That's how they operate. The people have a normal job, and then they'll also be working for intelligence part-time. And they'll get a lot of money for what they do.

Both Doctors, Derossi and Marino, were working for intelligence. It took them 43 minutes to deliver Diana to the hospital.

So, there was a very long period of time when she was in their care. At the inquest, one of the issues was that the healthcare system is different in Paris, and it is different, that's true.

In the U.S., it is called "scoop and run," when a person is in a car crash and injured, the ambulance rushes to the scene and picks up the victim, and rushes them to the hospital. In Paris and in France, what they have is a system that there's a doctor onboard the ambulance, and they have more equipment in the ambulance. So, the ambulance arrives at the crash scene, and they try to stabilize the patient. Then, they take them to the hospital.

But even in France, there are times when they will rush the person to the hospital. It depends on what the perception of the injuries is. If you've got a patient who is in Diana's situation, considering what she had been through, she had been in a 60 mile an hour car crash and wasn't wearing a seat belt, so her body was swung around 180 degrees, and she ended up on the floor with her back against the back of the front seat, and her legs up on the back seat. The thing is, doctors know that when you're involved in a crash like that, there could be some sort of internal injuries. It took 20 minutes from when the ambulance arrived to get her out of the car. Then, she got into the ambulance at 1:06 a.m., which was already 43 minutes after the crash. Once in the ambulance, they examined her. They saw she had bruises on the chest, and her blood pressure had dropped to 70. So, they knew at that stage that she had an injury they could not deal with in the ambulance. And that's the issue.

We have the transcripts from the base, and even they were asking the ambulance when they were leaving. The ambulance stayed in the tunnel for one hour and one minute. The other thing that you can see from the transcripts is that Doctor Derossi, who is the one phoning the base, said nothing to the base about Diana having a thoracic trauma. So, they didn't have a cardiac expert on hand to deal with Diana. If they had told the base that there was a thoracic trauma, then the base would have told the hospital what they needed.

Thoracic trauma is broadly categorized by mechanism into blunt or penetrating trauma. The most common cause of blunt chest trauma is motor vehicle collisions, which account for up to 80% of injuries. Other causes include falls, vehicles striking pedestrians, acts of violence, and blast injuries. Many patients with chest trauma die after reaching the hospital. Less than 10% of all blunt thoracic injuries require a thoracotomy, and many potentially life-threatening conditions can be relieved by simple procedures, such as chest tube insertion. Thus, many cases of traumatic deaths due to chest injury may be prevented by prompt diagnosis and a standardized therapeutic approach in the emergency room.

The other thing was that just before the ambulance got to the hospital, they stopped. There were two gentlemen who witnessed it. They witnessed a rocking ambulance. They also witnessed the driver coming out of the front and going into the back. They already had three people in the back. They had the doctor and two student interns. So, they ended up with four people in the back. This was just 500 yards from the hospital, and they never gave an explanation for why they stopped for five minutes.

The witnesses saw the ambulance rocking, so what were they doing? They said that they stopped the ambulance to give a cardiac massage and to increase the fluids because they thought that she might have a cardiac arrest. But she never had a cardiac arrest at that time.

When she got to the hospital, she only survived for another six minutes. So, the focus must be on what happened in the ambulance. Why did she die right after arriving at the hospital?

Q. Trevor Reese-Jones survived the crash and claims that he has no real memory of the accident. What are your thoughts on that?

A. Yes. He's changed his statement a few times. His evidence is very unreliable. I think that there are issues with the bodyguards – both Rees and the bodyguard at the hotel. The bodyguards were also at the same table as Henri Paul when he was drinking alcohol, so they shouldn't have allowed him to drive. They never did that. They both claimed that he was drinking pineapple juice, but they knew he was drinking Ricard. They both would have lost their jobs if they admitted they knew that Henri Paul was drinking the day before they left the hotel.

The whole idea of Henri driving the car was a bit unusual anyway because he had never actually driven during his 11 years at the hotel. When he went out to the airport that day, that was the first time he had ever driven for the hotel. He only had the luggage with him on the trip from the airport to the hotel. When he had the crash in the tunnel, that was the first time he had ever driven guests for the hotel.

I haven't studied the amnesia part yet of Trevor Rees-Jones, but it's something I need to do. The indication is that he may not have lost his memory because there's evidence from one of the housekeepers of his apartments in London. She said that she had spoken to Rees-Jones, and he told her not too long after the crash that if his memory came back, he would be in trouble.

Q. What more can you tell us about the driver Henri Paul?

A. He worked for the hotel, but the hotel was owned by Dodi's father, Mohamed Al-Fayed.

Q. But Mohamed Al-Fayed believes that his son, Dodi, and Diana were murdered and is offering a reward to find out the truth. Therefore, Henri Paul's boss didn't know that Paul was involved?

A. Yes, that's right. They have a different angle because they say that there's no way

Henri Paul worked for intelligence. But the evidence that Henri Paul worked for intelligence is very strong. It's pretty standard these days that in these high-class hotels, people working in their security department also works for intelligence, simply because intelligence has an interest in people that visit high-class hotels. But Henri Paul was receiving much more money than his wage the hotel was paying him. He had 17 bank accounts, and he had intelligence contacts in his address book. So, he was definitely working for intelligence.

Q. So who actually wanted her dead? Who is the one that made the order?

A. The evidence indicates that there are two motives. First, there's the involvement in the Anti-Landmine campaign. She had been to Angola in January 1997, and she had received a death threat over the phone from the Minister of the Armed Forces in the UK, Nickolas Soames.

Diana became embroiled in political controversy after fronting a Red Cross campaign to bring in an international ban on landmines at a time when the British government wanted an exemption for its forces.

Nicholas Soames, Tory MP for Mid-Sussex, has been a friend of Prince Charles since they were both boys. He went on television in November 1995 to denounce Diana as paranoid when she complained about people in the Prince's camp being out to get her. Soames then threatened Diana six months before her death and warned her to stop meddling in a controversy over landmines. Diana's friend Simone Simmons had listened in on a telephone conversation at the Princess's invitation in February 1997 and heard the then Armed Forces Minister warn her "accidents can happen." But Soames told an inquest that he had never made a threatening phone call to her or ever discussed the landmines issue with her. "It's a really grotesque suggestion," he said. Michael Mansfield, QC, cross-examining Soames on behalf of Mohamed Al-Fayed, told him that he had a very distinctive voice and that Ms. Simmons was sure it was he who made the threatening phone call.[8]

Then, in August, she went on another trip. This time to Bosnia. That was in the same month that she died. That trip was also part of her anti-landmines campaign, where she made a major speech about landmines. The fact is that Diana was a humanitarian, and if she had gotten the landmines banned, she would have moved onto something else.

The other motive technically involved Mohamed Al-Fayed, who was a longtime family friend of her father. In June of 1997, he offered her a holiday in his villa in the South of France, and she accepted that. But it wasn't just her that was going to be going on this holiday. She was going to be taking Prince William and Prince Harry. Now, Prince William was going to be the next King of England. The trip caused concern in the British establishment because Mohamed Al-Fayed was looked on as a man of ill repute. Just earlier that year, he had been involved in the "Cash-for-Questions" scandal with the government of the UK. So, he was looked upon as quite involved in the change of party. The royals were thought to have had a hand in this too.

In 1994, in what became known as the "cash-for-questions affair," Mohammed Fayed revealed the names of MPs he had paid to ask questions in parliament on his behalf, but who had failed to declare their fees. It saw the Conservative MPs Neil Hamilton and Tim Smith leave the government in disgrace, and a Committee on Standards in Public Life established to prevent such corruption from occurring again.

Fayed also revealed that the Cabinet Minister Jonathan Aitken had stayed for free at the Ritz Hotel in Paris at the same time as a group of Saudi arms dealers, leading to Aitken's subsequent unsuccessful libel case and imprisonment for perjury.

During this period, from 1988 to February 1998, Al-Fayed's spokesman was Michael Cole, a former BBC journalist, although Cole's PR work for Al-Fayed did not cease in 1998. Hamilton lost a subsequent libel action against Al-Fayed in December 1999 and a subsequent appeal against the verdict in December 2000. The former MP has always denied that he was paid by Al-Fayed for asking questions in parliament. Hamilton's libel action related to a Channel 4 Dispatches documentary broadcast on 16 January 1997 in which Al-Fayed made claims that the MP had received up to £110,000 in cash and received other gratuities for asking parliamentary questions. Hamilton's basis for his appeal was that the original verdict was invalid because Al-Fayed had paid £10,000 for documents stolen from the dustbins of Hamilton's legal representatives by Benjamin Pell.

Diana had been causing problems for the royals as well. Back in 1992, Andrew Morton released a biography in a book about her called *Diana: Her True Story*. Any royal reading it knew she was involved, even though her name wasn't mentioned. But it was obvious that she was collaborating, and she provided information about the inside workings of the royals and her mistreatment by the royals. That really upset the Queen. Others received some very strong letters from Phillip within ten days. Then, in 1995, Diana went on television, and what she had said in the book, she now said on TV. That was more of a very full-on situation than just being an unnamed collaborator of a book.

After that, in December, the Queen sent Diana a letter telling her that she and Charles should get a divorce, and that's what they did in August of 1996. But the Queen took it a lot further than just a divorce. She actually divorced her from the whole royal family and removed her HRH title. Once the Queen had done that, then she was outside of the royal circle.

When Diana had gone to Mohamed Al Fayed's villa, she met his son Dodi, and that's where they struck up a relationship. When the relationship continued after the holiday, that was another thing that the royals didn't like. Her death happened only three days after the conclusion of that holiday.

Q. Why would the French be involved?

A. Why would they support the royal family? They wouldn't. So, why are the French involved? It's because of the landmines. Arms are a huge sector of the French government. That's why they would get on-board. The same goes for Tony Blair and Bill Clinton. It's interesting that Bill Clinton made an announcement while Diana was still alive that he was signing an anti-landmine treaty on the 7th of September. After the crash when Diana died, Bill Clinton made another statement saying that they had reversed the decision, and the U.S. would not be signing the treaty.

President Clinton announced that the United States would not sign a treaty supported by nearly 100 other nations to ban the use of anti-personnel land mines. The United States had offered to sign the treaty only if it was amended to allow the continued use of land mines along the tense border between North and South Korea for at least 19 more years and to allow the use of anti-personnel mines in conjunction with anti-tank mines. Mr. Clinton insisted on the exemptions at the urging of the Defense Department, which warned that the United States would invite disaster on the Korean Peninsula if it removed the nearly one million land mines that seed the border between the two Koreas.[9]

Q. At the beginning of the interview, you mentioned Diana's letter thinking that she was going to be killed in a car accident. Who did she suspect was going to kill her?

A. She gave that note that I mentioned earlier to her butler. Also, in the same month, she had a meeting with her lawyer about her divorce. At the end of the meeting, she told her lawyer that she expected to die in an organized car crash. He had actually gone home that night, wrote a note, and locked it in his safe.

So, there were two notes of which she was fearful. In the first note, it actually named her husband, and in 1995, that was Charles. When she talked to the lawyer, there was no name mentioned. But when she spoke with people, she sort of feared that it would be MI6 that would do her in. But basically on the instructions of the senior royals or the establishment.

Listen to the full interview with John Morgan on my website:

https://www.alanrwarren.com/
hom-podcast-episodes/
episode/5eefe8c1/princess-
diana-death-john-morgan-
2014

Interview with Alan Power

I interviewed Alan Power one day after John Morgan in 2014. I had no idea about the conflict between the two of them until I talked with them. In such cases, it's easy for an author to blame unidentifiable people as the culprit by naming them as a group such as the CIA or MI6.

Anything that happens to them after they publish their book can be therefore blamed on the same group, making the author look like they are not only a true patriot by exposing the truth, but they are in danger for doing so.

Here is the bio that Alan Power sent to us for the show:

"Author Alan Power is married to Sally and has enjoyed a variety of interests, including being a drama student, an official candidate of the Conservative party, and owning his own company, but this is his first journey into the world of writing.

He has written another book about Diana that will be published later and has ideas for other subjects that will also follow. When his company suffered the ravages of internal fraud with no joy from the police due to lack of evidence and a degree of police indifference, his life changed irrevocably, but now he had the time to write.

When Diana was murdered, Alan remembers feeling rage that such a beautiful and natural person as Diana could be used, abused, and so cruelly discarded just to serve the monarchy's needs. He considered the probability that this was a murder of convenience and monarchical survival, so he began an extensive investigation into Diana's death.

Although initially unsure he would be up to this task, he persevered and now offers evidence that this murder was not conducted by rogue MI6 officers, considered as possible during the inquests, but by serving MI6 officers and with the use of military aid.

This project began in 2003, and despite many attempts by others to prevent or delay the book's release, Alan now brings you his findings. There is first an overview of the background to this brutal act and a selection of relevant events prior to the inquests, with lateral thought being applied to four million words of cross-referenced inquest evidence. He delivers the most compelling and damming evidence and says that it's important for justice to prevail if Britain still wishes to be considered a democracy." [10]

Q. What got you to write about this case?

A. One thing that really annoys me intensely was the state of the British nation and the monarchy, and the fact that they were treating Diana Spencer and then the issue when she was murdered. I was so enraged by it I thought something had to be done about it. Then, I thought, what can I do about it? Then, I thought if everyone said that, nothing would ever happen, so I gave it a go. I started it in November of 2003, and I just went flat out researching details, interviewing people, and by 2006, I had written the nonfiction side of it. It's a strange mix. The first half of the book is nonfiction, and the second is a story from, in my view, what happened.

Then, in 2007, the inquest was coming out. So, I had to spend a lot more time researching that to add to the evidence I already had. It gave me a chance to assess what happened during the inquest, what I knew had happened before, and the issues or the points that they hadn't brought out at the inquest. Also, the main points that they ignored, which gave me a lot more clout to write my book.

Q. How was it researching a case like Diana's death? How were people's responses to you while investigating?

A. By in large, very well. Most of the witnesses didn't like what happened any more than I did. But it was a very difficult position because they witnessed events take place, and they obviously had some pressure on them not to respond in too cold of a way. I think it's fair to say this. I had one, for example, the Japanese confidentially doing some work. And I was fairly sure I could get some of these witnesses to come along and talk to us, get on camera, and be on Japanese television. But I couldn't get one single witness to take part.

Q. Why is that? What was the fear behind it?

A. Basically, I think it was intimidation on the part of the British police and indeed the French. They were just controlling the whole thing. They clamped down on the whole thing. It was not to be released what happened or who had been responsible for her death. They intimidated people. I have been intimidated myself. They try to intimidate people from taking a risk. It didn't work on me, but it has worked on a lot of other people.

Q. How do you think the plan came about to kill Princess Diana?

A. My personal view is, it's pretty clear to me that the nod came from the palace to MI6 to continue with the assassination.

Q. Why do you think that Diana had to be killed?

A. There are a lot of reasons that people have come up with. Such as the landmine situation and being a nuisance all throughout the world. In the arms industry, and the cash that they were making from the arms industry. Perhaps there's some truth in that. But the main central reason that the monarchy was involved was that Diana had been abused since the beginning. Charles was even shacking up with Camilla Parker Bowles. She was just used for one particular purpose. She knew that. Obviously, not at the time. But later on, she did.

Camilla Parker Bowles, Duchess of Cornwall, is a member of the British royal family. She received her title upon her marriage to Charles, Prince of Wales, heir apparent to the British throne, on 9 April 2005. It is a second marriage for both of them. Despite being entitled to be known as Princess of Wales, she uses the title Duchess of Cornwall, her husband's secondary designation. In Scotland, she is known as the Duchess of Rothesay. Camilla was periodically romantically involved with the Prince of Wales both before and during their first marriages. The relationship became highly publicized in the media and attracted worldwide scrutiny.[11]

Once Harry was born, that was it. Her job was done. She said that when Harry was born, Charles was at the hospital with her. And as soon as he was born, he left. She knew at that moment he had gone to be with his baby. That was it. It was over. He had done his job, his duty, and the children were there.

Then, of course, she got very annoyed by it. And she was very independent, a very strong individual, and she wasn't going to put up with it. She had lots of evidence about what they had been getting up to at the palace. All of the "sexploits."

She made up a thick dossier on this. She had two copies of it. She gave one copy to her friend Simone Simons. Simone got nervous, unfortunately, and said she destroyed it after it being under her mattress for about one month. She was very nervous about what was going on behind the scenes and after Diana was murdered.

Simone Simmons, a healer by profession, formed a friendship with Diana. They met almost every day and spent several hours on the telephone. Diana told Simone she wanted her to write a book that revealed the truth about her. Simone wrote the book *Diana: The Last Word*, about her time counseling the princess.

Princess Diana's psychic has revealed the tragic royal's final secrets and released never-before-heard answerphone messages she left before her untimely death 23 years ago. According to Simone, Diana

- Was preparing to name and shame a mob of dangerous international arms dealers the morning of her untimely death,
- Wanted to move to America like Meghan Markle to escape the limelight and wanted to buy actress Julie Andrews' home in LA,
- Wasn't in love with her Dodi Fayed when she died and was instead intent on reuniting with her heart surgeon lover Hasnat Khan,
- Opened up to her about her deepest sex

secrets – including her hatred of making love to men with hairy backs,

• Recruited ex-rugby player Will Carling to give her a personal training program that would get rid of her bulimia-ravaged body and give her curves.[12]

So, I think that was the prime reason for it. Also, the police then sometimes tried to track down this dossier by searching all of the homes.

Q. Was the driver Henri Paul involved?

A. No. Henri Paul was basically conned into running the show. He was basically a very loyal servant and employee of the Ritz Hotel under Dodi. He did his job looking after them, driving them around occasionally just to help out. No, he certainly wasn't involved, and he was known to have been cooperative. He was ex-military, and he was used to doing what he was told.

He was structured by MI6 to set the whole thing in motion – to be where they wanted to be, and use the car they chose. They chose the particular car without tinted windows. They got him to drive it instead of using their daily chauffeur. They knew he would drive and instructed him to take that particular route. They had to enter the tunnel. Otherwise, there would have been no assassination.

But I think that Henri Paul was also a target because he would know what they were telling him to do and who was telling him to do it. If he survived, then he could give some pretty serious evidence against them.

The Secret Intelligence Service, commonly known as "MI6," is the foreign intelligence service of the United Kingdom, tasked mainly with the covert overseas collection and analysis of human intelligence in support of the UK's national security. Formed in 1909 as a section of the Secret Service Bureau specializing in foreign intelligence, the section experienced dramatic growth during

World War I and officially adopted its current name around 1920.

The name "MI6," meaning Military Intelligence, Section 6, originated as a flag of convenience during World War II when SIS was known by many names. It is still commonly used today.

The stated priority roles of MI6 are counterterrorism, counter-proliferation, providing intelligence in support of cybersecurity, and supporting stability overseas to disrupt terrorism and other criminal activities. Unlike its main sister agencies, the Security Service, known as "MI5," and Government Communications Headquarters, known as "GCH," MI6 works exclusively in foreign intelligence gathering and allows it to carry out operations only against persons outside the British Islands.[13]

Q. Dodi Fayed, did they want him dead as well?

A. No. I think the number one target was Diana. She had got to go. I think the fact that he was in the car was, in fact, a bonus, and they could get the whole lot wiped out at once. I think the only one that wasn't really a target was Trevor Rees-Jones.

Q. What are your thoughts on the ambulance and doctors not attending to Diana properly?

A. There are a lot of situations where you can discuss that sort of thing. But the problem is what I've got, and all good investigators have, is that we can only put down the facts. All it is that we can prove and not stuff that you believe might be the case. So, when it came to the ambulance, frankly, there is no evidence. There are documents of who said what and who they said it to. But there is nothing really definitive, and you can draw conclusions. If you want to put down opinions as facts to make a story, then I guess you can. I'm not prepared to do that. That's not investigative.

Listen to the full interview with Alan Power on my website:

https://www.alanrwarren.com/
hom-podcast-episodes/
episode/733d763e/alan-
power-princess-diana-death-
2014

Interview Afterthoughts

The world went into shock when Princess Diana died in the car crash in Paris. As the news came across the Tv's nobody could believe that she would die, how could she, she was the Princess of England. Probably just as the generation of the 1960's couldn't believe that John F. Kennedy, president of the United States was killed, there has to be some powerful conspiracy behind their death.

Just as the president of the United States could not be killed by a loser like Lee Harvey Oswald, there was no way she was killed by her drunk driver running from the paparazzi. How could someone so well protected and loved by the masses be killed by something as simple as a car crash?

There seems to be a thought that celebrities and politicians are untouchable and could never die as easily or simply as the common people living in the world. This kind of thinking allows us to look for something more, something much larger than us. It has to be a group that is even above the monarchy or presidents of the world.

This, along with the creative thinking of the hardcore believers of powerful elite groups such as the illuminati or deep state, can turn a simple car accident into a well plotted out murder of a monarch or leader of a free country.

Diana's death probably would have settled down in the media and went away faster, only Mohamed Al-Fayed, the father of her boyfriend at the time of her death, Dodi Fayed, who also died in the car crash, believed the accident was really a sophisticated murder of his son and Diana.

This was a catalyst to not only a tabloid sensation of scandal involving the royal family of England, but all of the conspiracy writers around the world. Two of these writers Alan Power and John Morgan led that pack and so involved they would write books claiming the other was a fraud.

We did several other interviews covering the subject, and they all told much the same story. Again, like the previous conspiracies in this book, they liked to blame the illuminati or deep state, and having the British Monarchy involved made it even more salacious.

Bottom line, the Queen of England didn't like Diana, especially after she divorced her son, Prince Charles and to make matters worse, she was now dating a rich and powerful Arab from Egypt. This is why the Queen had Diana killed? That's one of the major theories, but again, simply no evidence at all.

The other major theory is that the CIA had her murdered because she was travelling around the world and getting countries to ban the use of land mines. This was a big loss in money for these agencies, so she had to be stopped.

Those were the main motives and culprits behind the murder, but how did they do it?

Nobody really had any good evidence of a planned murder, but there was enough mystery involved to create a great crime fiction novel.

The conspiracy theorists start by making the ambulance drivers evil, they didn't do the correct procedure, and took their time getting to the hospital on purpose, in order to let her die. They must have been involved somehow, perhaps CIA.

Then Henri Paul the driver, he wasn't really drunk, he drank the same amount almost every night, so he could handle his booze. Except for his blood alcohol was three times the legal limit. It's also easy to say that the bodyguard in the front passenger seat of the car, that lived was involved. After all he claimed to have amnesia and that couldn't be true. In fact, they claim there was no such thing as amnesia.

Bottom line: It was a terrible accident, when the driver who was too drunk to hand the car at the speed he was going, while being chased by paparazzi crashed. All the evidence says that and nothing more. This was not murder.

1. CNN.com - "Diana letter 'warned of car plot' - Oct. 20, 2003" http://www.cnn.com/2003/WORLD/europe/10/20/diana.letter/index.html

2. https://en.wikipedia.org/wiki/Mohamed_Al-Fayed

3. Mohamed Al Fayed - Alchetron, The Free Social Encyclopedia. https://alchetron.com/Mohamed-Al-Fayed

4. https://en.wikipedia.org/wiki/Dodi_Fayed

5. Henri Paul | Gyaanipedia Wiki | Fandom. https://gyaanipedia.fandom.com/wiki/Henri_Paul

6. Henri Paul - Alchetron, The Free Social Encyclopedia. https://alchetron.com/Henri-Paul

7. https://en.wikipedia.org/wiki/Trevor_Rees-Jones_(bodyguard)

8. "'Accidents can happen': Warning to Diana from Prince ...." https://www.express.co.uk/news/uk/28297/Accidents-can-happen-Warning-to-Diana-from-Prince-Charles-s-friend

9. "Clinton Still Firmly Against Land-Mine Treaty - The New ...." https://www.nytimes.com/1997/10/11/world/clinton-still-firmly-against-land-mine-treaty.html

10. https://www.facebook.com/AlanPowerAuthor

11. https://en.wikipedia.org/wiki/Camilla,_Duchess_of_Cornwall

12. "Princess Diana pal shares haunting unheard messages and ...." https://www.dailystar.co.uk/news/latest-news/princess-diana-pal-shares-haunting-22670578

13. https://en.wikipedia.org/wiki/Secret_Intelligence_Service

References

All interviews were taken from the the *House of Mystery Radio Show* between 2010 and 2020. The show airs on several radio stations throughout the United States, including

- KKNW 1150 A.M. in Seattle/Tacoma,
- KCAA 106.5 F.M. in Los Angeles,
- KCAA 102.3 F.M. Riverside,
- KCAA 1050 A.M. Palm Springs,
- KFNX 1100 A.M. Phoenix,
- KFNX 540 A.M. Salt Lake City,
- on my website: *alanrwarren.com/house-of-mystery-radioshow*

Below is a list of our guests and their works in reference to the Conspiracy Theory Culture:

1. Alan Power: *Exposed: The Princess Diana Conspiracy - Revised Edition: The Evidence of Murder*, ASIN: B00JG2GDK4, Probity Press Ltd, April 2, 2014.
2. John Morgan: *How They Murdered Princess*

Diana: The Shocking Truth, ASIN: B00R6WH4P4, December 17, 2014.

3. Paul Davids: *Marilyn Monroe Declassified*, ASIN: B01LBIHPCU, September 27, 2016.

4. Gerrard Williams & Simon Dunstan: *Grey Wolf: The Escape of Adolf Hitler*, ISBN: 978-1402796197, Sterling, March 5, 2013.

5. Mark Sargent: *Flat Earth Clues: The Sky's the Limit*, March 23, 2016.

6. Marcus Allen: *No Evidence of Moon Landing*, Nexus News magazine Volume 22, July 2015.

7. Michael Murphy: *What in the World are they Spraying?*, DVD, 2020.

8. Michael Murphy: *Why in the World are they Spraying?*, DVD, 2012.

9. Rebekah Roth: *Methodical Illusion*, KTYS Media, ASIN: B00PREI4Y8, November 17, 2014.

10. Robert B. Stinnett: *Day of Deceit: The Truth About FDR and Pearl Harbor*, Free Press, ASIN: B000FBJHTO, December 14, 1999.

About Alan R. Warren

Alan R. Warren has written several bestselling True Crime books and has been one of the hosts and producers of the popular NBC news talk radio show the *House of Mystery,* which reviews True Crime, History, Science, Religion, Paranormal mysteries that we live with every day. From a darker, comedic, and logical perspective, he has interviewed guests such as Robert Kennedy Jr., F. Lee Bailey, Aphrodite Jones, Marcia Clark, Nancy Grace, Dan Abrams, and Jesse Ventura. The show is based in Seattle on KKNW 1150 AM and syndicated on the NBC network throughout the United States, including on KCAA 106.5 FM Los

Angeles/Riverside/Palm Springs, as well in Utah, New Mexico, and Arizona.

Read more about Alan on his website:
www.alanrwarren.com

f **BB** **g**

About Dr. Joseph Uscinski

Dr. Joseph Uscinski is an Associate Professor of Political Science at the University of Miami. He studies public opinion and mass media, with a focus on conspiracy theories and related misinformation.

He is coauthor of *American Conspiracy Theories* (Oxford, 2014) and editor of *Conspiracy Theories and the People Who Believe Them* (Oxford, 2018).

Read more about Dr. Joseph Uscinski on his website:
www.joeuscinski.com/

Also in The House of Mystery Interviews Series

The *House of Mystery Radio Show* has been on the air for ten years, broadcasting in over a dozen cities in the U.S. It started as a way to interview guests knowledgeable in many of the world's mysteries involving crime, science, religion, history, paranormal, conspiracies, etc. The House of Mystery Interview series is a curated collection of interviews from the show. Each volume focuses on one of the mysteries, providing the background and reproducing the main points discussed in the interviews. There will be no committed answer at the end, as the Interviews series does not attempt to solve the case. Instead, it provides the most compelling aspects of each theory held by different experts. This series is an excellent reference for researchers and a good overview for those unfamiliar with the case. Online links to the actual interviews are included.

VOLUME 1: JACK THE RIPPER: THE INTERVIEWS

Volume 1 of the Interview Series, "Jack the Ripper," covers the ultimate "who-done-it" mystery of 1888 London. Scotland Yard's "Whitechapel Murder File," in which Jack the Ripper had a starring role, went cold before it could be solved. One hundred thirty-two years later, and the fascination with this cold case mystery continues. Ripperologists passionately debate suspects, opinions, research methods, and theories. Even which murder victims to include in the case is widely debated. Astonishingly, work continues, and today Ripperologists still find new clues that bring us closer to solving the mystery.

The mix of credible and diverse thinkers interviewed includes world-renowned historian Neil Storey, the Godfather of Ripper Research, Paul Begg, Ripperologists: Paul Williams, Tom Wescott, Adam Wood, and Steve Blomer. Michael Hawley contributes his unprecedented scientific approach to the case. Suspect Ripperologists Jeff Mudgett, whose great-great-grandfather was serial killer H.H. Holmes, weighs in, as does Russell Edwards, who believes he solved the mystery through DNA.

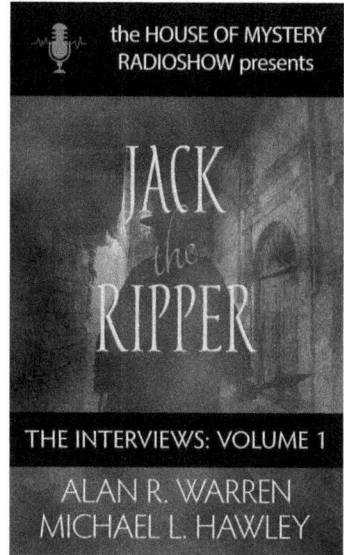

the HOUSE OF MYSTERY RADIOSHOW presents

JACK the RIPPER

THE INTERVIEWS: VOLUME 1

ALAN R. WARREN
MICHAEL L. HAWLEY

VOLUME 2: JFK ASSASSINATION: THE INTERVIEWS

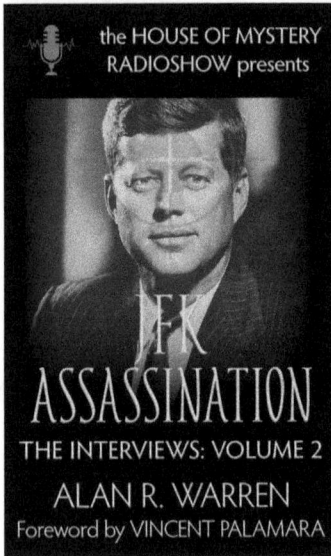

the HOUSE OF MYSTERY
RADIOSHOW presents

JFK
ASSASSINATION
THE INTERVIEWS: VOLUME 2
ALAN R. WARREN
Foreword by VINCENT PALAMARA

Volume 2 of the Interview Series, "JFK Assassination," covers *the* unrivaled historical mystery of historical mysteries. The JFK assassination is the grandfather of all conspiracies in America and arguably where they all started. A highly popular President with movie star looks and charisma, effecting significant changes in society, was brutally cut down in his prime. The official story was that JFK was killed by a sole assassin, Lee Harvey Oswald. However, many conspiracy theorists believe in an assassination plot involving the FBI, CIA, U.S. military, VP LBJ, Cuba's Fidel Castro, Russia's KGB, the Mafia, or some combination of those entities.

The research and interviewing of the JFK assassination experts lasted for over six years. Arguments and counter-arguments from a diverse mix of bestselling authors make for some interesting discussions. And some of the authors interviewed are considered just as controversial as the mystery itself. Most authors focused on who they believe was responsible for the assassination. Others narrowed their focus on certain related aspects, such as the Zapruder film, Nix film, Garrison Tapes, etc. All information collected from each expert adds value to the overall mystery.

VOLUME 3: ZODIAC KILLER: THE INTERVIEWS

Volume 3 of the Interview Series, "Zodiac Killer," covers another serial killer who has stayed in the spotlight for years after their case has gone cold. It's been over 40 years now, and fascination with the Zodiac is still going strong. Experts passionately debate Zodiac suspects, Zodiac''s letters/ciphers, opinions, and theories. Even which murder victims to include in the case is widely debated.

the HOUSE OF MYSTERY RADIOSHOW presents

WANTED

SAN FRANCISCO POLICE DEPARTMENT

ZODIAC KILLER

THE INTERVIEWS: VOLUME 3

ALAN R. WARREN
MICHAEL BUTTERFIELD

The diverse mix of authors interviewed includes cryptologist and cipher expert David Oranchak, authors who propose their suspects are already convicted serial killers, authors who claim the Zodiac was their father, authors who offer new or already considered suspects, and an author who argues the Zodiac killer didn't exist at all and that Zodiac was a hoax.

VOLUME 4: MYSTERIOUS CELEBRITY DEATHS: THE INTERVIEWS

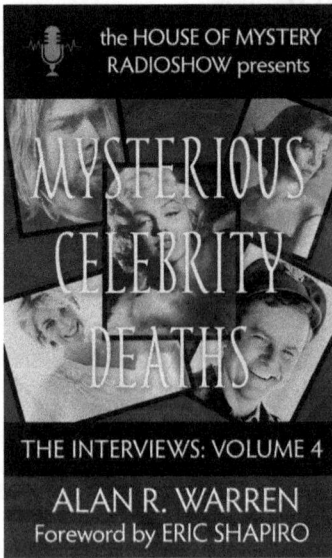

the HOUSE OF MYSTERY RADIOSHOW presents

MYSTERIOUS CELEBRITY DEATHS

THE INTERVIEWS: VOLUME 4

ALAN R. WARREN
Foreword by ERIC SHAPIRO

Volume 4 of the Interview Series, "Mysterious Celebrity Deaths," covers interviews relating to the mysterious deaths of the influential rock band Nirvana's frontman Kurt Cobain, the 1960s mega-icon Marilyn Monroe, TV's *Hogan's Heroes* lead actor Bob Crane, the talented and multi-award-winning actress Natalie Wood, and the people's princess, Princess Diana.

www.ingramcontent.com/pod-product-compliance
Lightning Source LLC
Chambersburg PA
CBHW062112020426

42335CB00013B/934